Sherry *A Life's Journey*

Philip Rowles

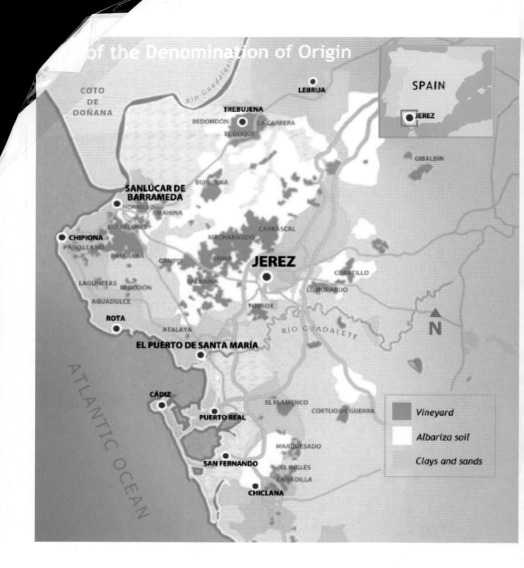

of the Denomination of Origin

COTO DE DOÑANA

LEBRIJA

TREBUJENA

REDONDÓN   LA CARRERA

EL DUQUE

SPAIN

JEREZ

GIBALBÍN

BURUENA

SANLÚCAR DE BARRAMEDA

HORNILLO   MAHINA

CARRASCAL

MIRAFLORES

MACHARNUDO

CHIPIONA

PAGOLLANO

PASTRANA

CAMPIX   AÑINA

JEREZ

CUARTILLO

LAGUNETAS   RECODÓN

BALBAINA

LOMOPARDO

AGUADULCE

TORROX

ROTA

ATALAYA

RÍO GUADALETE

N

EL PUERTO DE SANTA MARÍA

CÁDIZ

EL FLAMENCO

CORTIJO DE GUERRA

PUERTO REAL

MARQUESADO

SAN FERNANDO

EL INGLÉS

CAÑADILLA

CHICLANA

ATLANTIC OCEAN

Vineyard

Albariza soil

Clays and sands

Sherry *A Life's Journey*

Philip Rowles

This book is dedicated to the memory of:

Beltrán Domecq González, and his charming wife
Anne Christine Williams.

*Without their generosity and encouragement I would have
left Jerez much sooner, and this remarkable journey would
never have started.*

"If penicillin can cure those that are ill, Sherry can bring the
dead back to life."

Sir Alexander Fleming (1881 – 1955)
Discoverer of penicillin.

About the Author

Philip Rowles is by training a Spanish linguist, who came to be in the Wine Trade almost by accident, but has now been in that Trade for almost 50 years. Following his formative years at Williams & Humbert in Jerez he has worked in various capacities with several Sherry Bodegas, including González Byass, Garvey, Marqués de Real Tesoro and Lustau. He has also had strong commercial and oenological links with Bodegas Torres, C.V.N.E, Bodegas Ochoa and Freixenet.

He was principal lecturer at Diploma Level for the WSET on both Spanish Light Wines and Sherry for many years, and for his contribution to Spanish Wine Education was made a member of the Gran Orden de Caballeros del Vino in 1991. In the same year he was seconded to the E.U. in Brussels to help set up and roll out the fledgling E.U. Wine Inspectorate within the Agriculture Directorate. For the last 20 years of his working life he was Wine Manager at Freixenet U.K., overseeing the technical aspects of their extensive Spanish, Californian and South American portfolio.

Now semi-retired he has found time to return to his first wine love – Sherry; and to write this book.

Contents

Foreword

I remember, perhaps more clearly than for any other wine, the first time that I tried sherry. My parents owned a gastropub in the eighties, a time when these chalky, slate dry wines weren't celebrated to the extent that they are today. One of my holiday jobs in my teens was to set up the bar for morning opening hours. This, amongst other things, required setting the fires, stocking up the bottles, checking the beers on draught and the opened house wines from the night before. Finally, I had to place a huge brass fire-pot on the corner of the bar and fill it with ice and, without fail, one bottle of La Ina, Tio Pepe and La Gitana sherries, along with an assortment of French aperitifs. I must have looked at those bottles a thousand times before curiosity finally got the better of me and I tried them. That arresting, ice-cold, savoury, sourdough hit of a freshly-opened bottle of Fino left my neck-hairs standing on end. I'm not even sure whether, at that moment, I even liked it, but it started an intrigue and eventually a love affair with the amazing liquids of Jerez that has transcended any other wine fascination that I have enjoyed over the past thirty years.

It is an honour both to know Philip and to be asked to write this foreword. He knows everyone in the sherry industry and everyone knows him. I met him through the strangest of connections. A dear friend, Eleanor Smyly, who I met years ago, while going through the throes of my divorce, asked me if I had met her godfather 'Felipe'. He was a close friend of Eleanor's now dearly departed father, also named Philip, possibly the coolest man in London. I said I hadn't. On meeting Philip Rowles with Eleanor, I realised that I had already met him as a lecturer at the headquarters of the world-renowned Wine & Spirit Education Trust. He was the most charming, inspiring and eloquent of lecturers on a subject shrouded in ambiguity and complex law. On hearing that he was compiling a definitive book on the topic of sherry, I was excited. Philip not only knows everything about this endlessly diverse and magical wine, but he knows how to teach. The wine industry has been crying out for a book like this for two decades. It is clear, technically precise and extremely easy to read. It clears up many misunderstandings about the genre, fills in huge gaps in common understanding, including where and how the raw materials are grown, and what terms like 'Palo Cortado' actually mean (something that took me years to fully understand), and is wonderfully easy to read. I endorse this book wholeheartedly.

Joe Wadsack – Wine Journalist, T.V. Presenter and Blogger.

Introduction

Author's acknowledgements

I first went to Jerez in the autumn of 1969. I had just left college with a qualification in Business Studies and Modern languages, and was keen to gain some first hand experience in the language and culture of Spain. Even though I came from a family with strong links to the hotel industry, my knowledge of wine was – at best – limited.

Jerez was to change that in a most spectacular way!

I had intended to stay in Jerez for at the most six months, out of gratitude to the benefactor who had found me the placement, and then move on to another part of Spain.

Jerez, though had other ideas, and almost three years later I decided to move back to the UK, to work in – The Sherry Trade.

I had started at Williams & Humbert as a guide in their small visitors' section, and quite simply fell in love with the place and its wines!

My career from there has been varied, continuously in the wine trade, but somehow, always connected either directly or indirectly to Jerez and its wonderful wines.

I have been honoured to be able to lecture for the WSET at Diploma level on The Wines of Spain and Sherry for over 20 years, and hope that this book will be an encouragement to students in future years in understanding the complexities and pleasure of the wines of the Marco de Jerez.

There are many great intellectual works on this subject, whose insight of the historical detail and description of the origins of the Sherry Trade are much superior to mine. Among those I would count "Sherry" by Julian Jeffs, an initial source of inspiration, along with that of the late Manuel González Gordon, also entitled "Sherry".

In addition, there are various works by Beltrán Domecq Williams, who at the time of writing is now the President of the Consejo Regulador de Jerez – Xérès – Sherry, and who joined the family company – Williams and Humbert, straight from University in Madrid, at more or less the same time as I did. I have counted him as a lifelong friend ever since.

I cannot fail to mention here, the late and dearly missed John Radford, who I first met in Jerez in 1971 when he was working in a sales capacity for a UK wholesaler based in Nottingham. His book The New Spain has, I am sure, been a source of great pleasure for many a lover of Spanish wines.

My intention with this book is not to try to emulate any of those immensely learned works, but to set out for lovers and students of Sherry alike, a simplified and at the same time commercially focused account of how these wonderful wines are made, exploring their uniqueness, charms and mysteries in a way that will hopefully allow readers to take even further enjoyment from drinking them.

In addition to the four aforementioned gentlemen, I would like to thank the many more people who have been key players in my understanding and enjoyment of Sherry, and without whom I would not be where I am today, nor able to write this book. Some have been a part of the journey for many years, and others have been vital sources of information and wisdom in the recent research I have undertaken to bring this book to fruition. All of them I thank wholeheartedly. They are listed, in no particular order, at the back of the book, p.188.

1

A Short History

Setting the Scene

The wines of Jerez and its surrounding villages and vineyards can rightly lay claim to being rooted in the origins of Europe's oldest recorded products of vitis vinifera. The Phoenicians, in around 800BC, brought the original vines with them, from Asia Minor, as part of their commercialization of the region.

The Dona Blanca Ruins

Outside the town of El Puerto de Santa María can still be found the ruins of the village of Doña Blanca, which has been dated to around that time, and in which can plainly be seen the remains of an old wine press.

Jerez owes its development almost entirely to commerce and trade, from that date to the present day, and in that respect has great commonality with the classic wine trading regions of Bordeaux and Oporto.

The physical location of the Sherry Triangle, close to the Straits of Gibraltar – the mythical Pillars of Hercules, has meant that, from those ancient times, its lands have been criss-crossed by a host of different trading nations or states.

From those early days, the Phoenicians gave way eventually to the Greeks, whose God of Wine, Dionysius was claimed to have a particular fondness for the wines of the region, and then to the Romans, who called the town we now know as Jerez "Ceret", so creating the beginning of its currently recognizable name. The wine of Ceret was much prized in Rome, and evidence exists that its price was far in excess of any wine produced locally. Following the fall of Rome, the first centuries A.D. are, in common with much of the rest of southern Europe, best referred to as the Dark Ages.

However in 711 A.D. the region was invaded by the Moors, as the final piece in their cultural and trade domination of the western Mediterranean basin. They renamed the town

Seris, and although wine consumption was prohibited by Koranic teachings, grape growing continued to flourish, both for winemaking and for raisins. The area was retaken by the Christian King of Castille in 1264, and was named Jeres, a recognisable version of its current name; the word Frontera being added almost a century later – the word Frontera being Spanish for frontier, denoting its location at the frontier between Christian and Muslim territories.

The growth in Sherry production and sales, both domestic and export in the following centuries was exponential, with British, Irish and Flemish traders all beginning to deal in the wines, and when, in 1492 the Americas were discovered, the ships which sailed in those adventures were built in the region, and, importantly supplied with its wines for the journey.

By that time as well, the two towns of El Puerto de Santa María and Sanlúcar de Barrameda had been fully absorbed into the winemaking fabric of the region, and the trading area we now know as the Sherry Triangle had been fully formed and was one of the most important wine producing regions of the Iberian Peninsula.

12th.C Moorish Map of the region by Al Idrisi

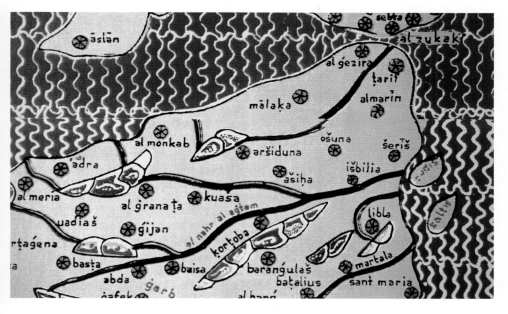

The Sherries of the time would have been very different to those we know today, in that there was only one really stand out style – a full bodied, highly fortified sweet wine – known at the time as Sack. The word has nothing to do with sacking material, but much more likely has its origins in the Spanish word "sacar" to take out (or to export), as we find it in the same period being used to describe wines such as Malaga Sack and Canary Sack.

Falstaff in HENRY IV Part 2 by
William Shakespeare

"If I had a thousand sons, the first humane principle I would teach them should be, to forswear thin potations, and to addict themselves to Sack"

Fino and the styles onwards to Amontillado and Palo Cortado had really not yet been popularised, although there is anecdotal evidence that wines of these styles were drunk locally, especially in the towns, villages and hamlets closer to the coast of the Bay of Cadiz. Wines exported would principally be those of a single vintage, perhaps two at most, blended across the region. Present day structures and production methods were not yet in place.

Trade in the wines of the region was the mechanism which started to develop and evolve what we have today in terms of viticulture, wine making, and most importantly the system of fractional blending used as the basis for the Solera system. Sherry sales were beginning to burgeon throughout Europe. Customers were looking for consistency of both quality and style, and it was no longer seen as sufficient to offer wines which varied in those parameters.

Winery owners and distributors started to recognize that the unique characteristics of the soils, topography, grape varieties and climate of the Sherry region could produce consistent wines of a variety of styles, using a system which seems to have come about almost by accident.

The drivers of this change of style were almost exclusively in-comers to the region, merchants mainly, but not always originally trading in wine. The 17th. and 18th. Centuries saw the arrival in the region of names such as Mackenzie, Garvey, Gordon, Williams and Humbert, Sandeman and many more, who would over time become stalwarts of Sherry production and commercial development.

As well as exporting to Europe, many of these producers would start to develop the already existing connections between Spain and the Americas, and by the end of the 19th. Century, Sherry was a universally known drink.

It is not fully documented when, where or how what we now take for granted as the Solera system with its feeder nurseries – Criaderas came to be. But that it came to be bears testament to the skill, patience and vision of those pioneers.

A famous treatise dated 1807, written by Esteban Boutelou, one of Spain's first ever recorded ampelographers, concerning the vines, grapes and wines of Jerez and Sanlucar de Barrameda, makes absolutely no reference to either Soleras or Criaderas. In fact, the first reference to them in the inventories of the old House of Garvey appears in 1849.

The mid to late 19th. Century and the first half of the 20th. Century was to be a golden age for Sherry production and sales.

Spain's first wine related Regulatory Council, the Consejo Regulador was constituted in 1933, to regulate and set in place the viticultural and winemaking regulations, as well as setting down the permitted labelling and marketing practices by which Sherry could be made and traded. This was followed by Consejos Reguladores being established in all Spain's quality winemaking regions and was the fore-runner of the system of the viticultural and winemaking control bodies in place today. The Consejo's Council is made up of 10 representatives of growers, and 10 representatives of winemakers and shippers all of whom are elected and/or re-elected on a four yearly basis. As well as compiling the rule book, the Consejo also took the step of meticulously recording all manner of statistics, and still does to this day.

The most telling are the first export statistics, which date from the late 1930s, and show shipments at almost 250,000 hectolitres, a staggering figure then, equivalent to 2¾ million 9 litre cases. The figure, quite naturally dropped

Horse Racing on the beach at Sanlúcar

during and just after World War 2, but had staged a good recovery by 1960, when the figure was around 300,000 hectolitres. Thereafter Sherry boomed worldwide, rising through 700,000 hl. in 1969 up to 1,500,000hl in 1979. This was a peak, and the world of wine drinking was changing. Sherry was associated with things old fashioned, and the post war generation wanted more exciting wines.

The following 10 years showed a 50% decline to just over 770,000 hl. It was a very difficult time in the industry, with many jobs lost, and many Bodegas either closed or were taken into the ownership of multinational companies.

It is, I suggest, reasonable to argue that the Sherry industry was the architect of its own demise. Rather than trying to compete with a vast array of quality light wines from around the world on quality terms, it seemed to be driving headlong into the concept of cheap branding and chasing market share. Competition was deemed to be purely other Sherries, wines of similar characteristics from less expensive places of production, and products such as vermouth. Sherry was in complacent mode. It had been Spain's most successful wine region for centuries, and was now expanding at an alarming rate. It was prosperous

The 17th. C Jerez Cathedral

and could not see its own problems. There was too much poor quality wine being produced, much of it dependent on subsidies of one sort or another, and much of it moved around the world only on paper.

One of the principal protagonists of the decline, and of Sherry's problems, although not the only one was a multinational business named RUMASA.

It had its origins as a Sherry Almacenista Bodega called Zoilo Ruiz-Mateos dating back to the mid 19th. Century, and began to ship wine under its own brand name in the 1950s, and in 1958 started to supply Harveys of Bristol Ltd with most of their Sherry, especially Bristol Cream, in 1964 signing a contract with them to be their exclusive supplier for the following 100 years. Although the contract was rescinded soon afterwards following the takeover of Harveys by another UK drinks producer, Ruiz-Mateos continued to be a major supplier and the family amassed considerable wealth.

At about this time José María Ruiz-Mateos, son of Zoilo took charge of the company and embarked on a business plan of considerable expansion, mainly by means of take-overs, not only of other Sherry houses, but also of banks, hotels, construction companies and other winemaking businesses throughout Spain. It became an enormous business enterprise, and at one stage it was calculated that its annual turnover was somewhere close to 2% of Spain's GDP.

The Sherry Bodegas they acquired included Williams and Humbert, Pemartín, Diez Mérito, Garvey, Bertola, Lacave, Vergara & Gordon, Varela and Bertola. By the late 1970s, RUMASA dominated Sherry, both in production, sales and most importantly pricing. They consolidated production in both vineyard and winery and drove export prices inexorably downwards, whilst at the same time pushing for expanded vineyard planting through their increasing domination of the votes within the Consejo Regulador.

RUMASA was taken into government ownership by the newly elected Socialist government in 1983, claiming that it owed millions in unpaid taxes, was effectively insolvent, moving money around its banks at below the market rate levels of interest, and if it were allowed to continue the Spanish economy could have been irreparably damaged. Given the GDP percentage, and in addition the fact that RUMASA directly employed in the region of 100,000 people throughout Spain, as well as being indirectly responsible for secondary and tertiary levels of labour, it was indeed a brave move.

Perhaps there was no need. Nothing has ever been officially published to fully justify it on grounds of financial probity, and J.M. Ruiz Mateos was eventually acquitted by the Spanish Supreme Court in 1999. He was however something of a "Brand Bandit", and from personal experience, a megalomaniac. But the exponential growth of the business during the 1970s especially, its appropriation and the resulting sell off changed the face of Sherry making and marketing in a way that is only now being fully understood and addressed.

Very quickly the government moved to sell off all the Sherry bodega elements of its appropriation to existing Sherry Houses, but the region was shell shocked and there were many negative effects. One of the worst was a substantial increase in unemployment following the necessary restructuring of the old RUMASA bodegas within the now much smaller core of the industry. There was much unrest, and there were many recriminations, both on personal and commercial levels, ands old wounds took time to heal. Following disastrous strikes, loss of sales at home and in key export markets, a rescue plan was engineered by the Consejo Regulador. It dealt with the problems as they related to the size of the vineyard planted and also to the wineries stock levels and sales ratios. Over more than a 15 year period it has brought the industry back into some sort of balance, and it is once more finding its rightful place at the quality end of the market, whilst managing to retain its key, core everyday sales.

There have been many cases over the years of the word "Sherry" having been used by producers other than those in the Jerez region of Spain, and there have been many legal battles. Whilst these are vital to what we now have, they are not totally relevant to the aims of this book.

The topic will be dealt with separately in Appendix 1.

Traditional foot pressing – now only
seen ceremonially

2

Vineyards

Vineyards

The Sherry vineyards are located in what is known in Spanish as the "Marco de Jerez" – or Jerez Region, which is a particularly benevolent location in the extreme south west of Spain; most of them are in the Province of Cadiz, but some are situated within the boundaries of the Province of Seville, in the municipality of Lebrija. The vineyards are bounded by the Atlantic Ocean to the west, the mighty River Guadalquivir to the North West, and the lesser, but significant River Guadalete to the south and east. In addition, when one factors in the influence of the Sierra de Cadiz on the eastern extreme, (remarkably, the town of Ubrique in the centre of this mountain range has one of the highest annual average levels of rainfall in Spain), these boundaries create a unique geographical and climatological region within Lower Andalucía.

Here the purity and strength of the light, the relatively high, particularly propitious levels of rainfall, and the influences of the winds from both south east and south west combine with the unique soils, to create the perfect conditions for the grapes to grow and Sherry wines to be produced.

The Marco de Jerez

Jerez Superior and Jerez Zona

There are two distinct areas of vineyards recognized within the Marco de Jerez. The majority is known as Jerez Superior, and the balance Jerez Zona. As recorded in the 2016 Annual Report of the Consejo Regulador, there are currently 6,362.05 hectares registered in Jerez Superior and 626.94 in Jerez Zona. These are broken down into 2,367 distinct vineyard sites, scattered throughout the 9 distinct municipalities of the region, and these are registered, as at 1st. September 2016 to 1,642 separate vineyard owners.

Table 1

The following table gives the details of those vineyard locations and the average size of the holdings.

Municipality	Superior	Zona	Total ha.	No. Vineyards	Average Holding ha.
Chiclana	0.00	133.08	133.08	144	0.92
Chipiona	33.24	72.62	105.86	86	1.23
El Puerto de Santa María	260.90	6.20	267.09	57	4.69
Jerez de la Frontera	4645.35	0.78	4646.13	443	10.49
Lebrija	0.00	144.71	144.71	128	1.13
Puerto Real	0.00	121.97	121.97	32	3.81
Rota	94.65	46.67	141.31	53	2.67
Sanlúcar de Barrameda	784.28	36.18	820.46	600	1.37
Trebujena	543.64	64.72	608.36	824	0.74
Total	6262.05	626.94	6988.99	2367	–
				Average	2.95

As can be seen from Table 1, the average vineyard holding is tiny. Even factoring in the vast holdings of Bodegas such as Barbadillo (550 ha), Gonzalez Byass (800ha), Lustau (130ha), Estévez Group (800ha), Williams & Humbert (240ha) and the other major producers and shippers, very few of whom are self sufficient in grapes, it becomes apparent how important the role of the small independent growers and co-operatives is in delivering a balanced supply of grapes and musts to satisfy the needs of the bulk of Sherry producers and shippers.

In fact, some 42% of the vineyard is owned by members of one of the region's 7 co-operatives, 28% by independent growers, and 30% by people or organizations which are also registered Sherry Producers or Shippers.

The vineyard area has reduced by much more than half in the last 20 years, most of the reduction as a result of EU grubbing up subsidies, and stemming from the Industry's recognition in the late 1990s and the early years of the 21st. century, that the increases in plantings of the 70s and 80s had been excessive and were no longer relevant to the reduced scale of global trade in Sherry.

Jerez Vineyard Ownership

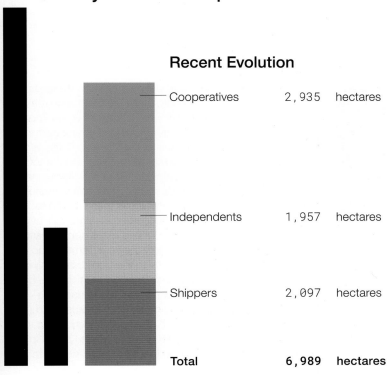

Recent Evolution

Cooperatives	2,935	hectares
Independents	1,957	hectares
Shippers	2,097	hectares
Total	**6,989**	**hectares**

1990   2016   2016

The exact figures of registered plantings in 1990 were:

Jerez Superior	12,417	hectares
Jerez Zona	5,477	hectares
Total	17,894	hectares

Data Source - C.R.D.O. Jerez –
Xérès – Sherry

The area planted in 1990 was almost three times the area of that planted today, with the percentage of plantings in the lower quality Zona areas now down almost ten fold. At that time Zona represented some 30% of the total vineyard, whereas now it is down to just a little under 9%.

Regulations state that at least 60% of the Palomino grapes used to make Sherry in any one vintage must be delivered from vineyards within the Jerez Superior sector. What is interesting to note is that the grapes used to create wines with protected Denomination of Origin status "Jerez-Xérès-Sherry", which must be aged within the municipal boundaries of Jerez and El Puerto de Santa María, as well as those used to create wines with protected Denomination of Origin status "Manzanilla-Sanlúcar de Barrameda", which must be aged within the municipal boundaries of Sanlúcar de Barrameda, can be grown anywhere within the demarcated Jerez Superior and Jerez Zona vineyards, so long as the 60% rule is adhered to.

Zona de Producción

To complicate matters a little, just as there are vineyards in Jerez Superior and Jerez Zona, there are base wine making Bodegas which are located in what is known as the Zona de Producción, or Production Zone. These are located in 4 municipalities which are not within the Zona de Crianza, in which Sherry must legally be matured. These are the towns of Chiclana de la Frontera, Chipiona, Rota and Trebujena. There are a total of 12 such Bodegas. Their role is twofold. Firstly they produce base wine which is then sold on to registered Bodegas de Crianza, located in Jerez, El Puerto or Sanlúcar, and which is then entitled to full denomination as Sherry or Manzanilla. Secondly they are permitted to sell their own aged wines directly to the public, but only designated as wine made in their specific municipality, but not as Sherry; although they are permitted to use style descriptors used for Sherry, such as Fino, Oloroso and Cream. Not surprisingly most of their aged and bottled production is sold locally, although one, César Florido in Chipiona does export, mainly Moscatel based wines, to several export markets.

To put these Bodegas into a little perspective, it is worth noting that in the 2016 vintage their total combined production was just under half a million litres of young wine, whereas the total production for the entire harvest that year was some 38.4 million litres.

Soils

As can be seen from Table 1 and the Map on p.2, the Title facing page, some 80% of the vineyards are located within the municipalities of Jerez, El Puerto and Sanlúcar, and in the area between the three towns. They are situated on the gently rolling hills, mainly on the tops of hills and on the slopes below. Even though there are hills, this is low lying land with the highest altitude something less than 350 feet above sea level. The predominant soil of the region is the famed albariza.

The white albariza soil has been dated back to the Tertiary Period, which lasted from around 66 million years ago to around 2 million years ago. It is rich in calcium carbonate, with a minimum of 25% and up to 40% active limestone, combined with a mixture of silica and clay derived from the diatomite and radiolite shells which were present in the Oligocene Sea which once covered the area. The finest of all the albariza soils are those with the highest proportion of limestone and silica, the remaining clay element acting as a binding agent to give albariza is famed water retention properties. Whilst chalky limestone is not unique to Jerez in the world of wine, what is certain is that Sherry could not be made without it!

The ability to retain moisture is one of the principal properties of Albariza soil. It is able to act rather like a sponge following the winter rain, creating a vast reservoir of moisture which will keep the vines nourished during the heat of summer. It also creates a solid cap on, or just under the surface in that summer heat, and which has the dual benefit of reflecting the sun's rays back through the vine to help the ripening process, but also preventing evaporation of the water content it holds below ground.

These factors also have a major influence on the yield of the vines, the characteristics of the grapes they ripen and thus the base wine produced. Notwithstanding the great heat of summer, the Jerez region is one of the highest yielding in Spain, at around 70 hl/ha – compared to around 35hl/ha in Rioja and just 23 hl/ha in La Mancha, which is equally as hot. The reasons for this are, primarily the previously mentioned water retention capabilities of the Albariza soils, but also the fact that the base wine for Sherry does not need anything like the flavour concentrations of other unfortified white wines in Spain, as the concentrations and complexities will be achieved through fortification initially, but more importantly through the complex Solera ageing processes which all Sherry passes through.

Albariza is visibly evident on the higher slopes, where the topsoil has been mainly eroded and washed down into the lower lying areas. These lower areas are now planted mainly with cereals, sunflowers and sugar beet, but are also home to some of the Zona vineyards, planted on this eroded soil, known as Barros, which literally translates as "muddy earth". A third type of soil found in the region is known as Arenas or Sand, and is logically to be found closer to the sea, principally around the towns of Chipiona and Chiclana. This is where the majority of the Moscatel grapes are grown, principally to be turned into sweetening wines.

The finest Albariza soils are located at elevations from 65m up to 90m, as can be seen highlighted in the diagram below:

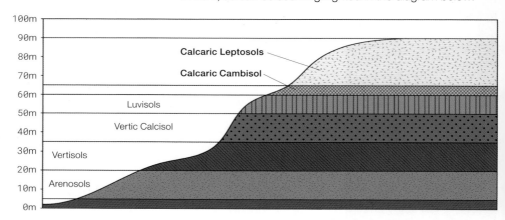

Data Source – C. Pardo Calle et al.

Pagos

The vineyards of Jerez are divided into specific delimited areas of land, known as Pagos, ranging from just a few hectares to several which have in excess of 800. Each has its own, specific, identifiable characteristics from those contiguous to it. The particular features of each derive from attributes such as orientation, exposure to sunlight, soil composition, location and microclimate. Each pago will produce wines of a definable character, which in turn will deliver measurable attributes to the finished wine derived from them.

Until recently there were 45 separate Pagos recognised by the Consejo Regulador, but in 2016, following extensive work undertaken by the Consejo, and based on detailed work by many diverse sources, including work published in 2011 by C. Pardo-Calle et. al. based at the University of Sevilla, this number was increased to 69. These have been identified by all the competent Regulatory Authorities as producing wines with such specific discernible characteristics as to warrant single vineyard site labelling in years to come, so long as traceability can be guaranteed. The legislation allows for wines created in the 2015 harvest and onwards to qualify for this status. The principal Pagos are Añina, Balbaina, Carrascal and Macharnudo close to Jerez; Miraflores, Pastrana, Torre Breva and Hornillo near to Sanlúcar; and Los Tercios along with Balbaina Baja, just inland from El Puerto.

There are, in fact two separate pagos named Carrascal. The first, and more important, with a maximum delimited area of 885 hectares, but only currently 403 planted to Sherry producing vines and which lies some 5km due north of Jerez, will be the one referred to in the rest of this book. The second has a delimited area of 159 hectares, with just under half currently planted to Sherry vines and is located 5km south of Sanlúcar and is of much less importance.

There is no hard or fast rule as to the styles of base wine produced out of each, but as a general rule of thumb, those closest to the sea and with southerly and/or westerly aspect, and at lower elevation will tend to produce lighter style musts, more likely to develop into Fino styles, including Manzanillas, whilst those further inland and at higher elevation, where days are hotter and the cooling sea breeze is less of an influence, will tend to produce heavier styles, be they heavier weight Finos which may eventually be turned into Amontillados or Palo Cortados; or wines destined from the very outset to be Olorosos.

However, it must be noted that Gonzalez Byass, the region's biggest producer of Fino and other biologically aged Sherries, has the majority of its vineyards, close to 800ha. in total planted in Macharnudo and Carrascal; and Barbadillo, the largest Manzanilla producer has 400ha. in Gibalbín, which is about as far as it is possible to plant vineyards from the coast. The most important issue here is that these vineyards are inclined towards the south west, and affected by the cooling, damper Poniente wind and protected from the harsher, negative effect of the searingly hot Levante wind.

3

Climate

Climate

The Jerez Region is located at a latitude of around 36° N, one of the most southerly vineyard areas in the northern hemisphere. The climate of the region is very special, and is one of the principal factors in determining Sherry as a wine. Put quite simply it is hot, as a direct consequence of its southerly latitude. However, it is also wet, due to its proximity to the Atlantic Ocean. In addition the fact that it is also low lying makes it particularly susceptible to the influences of the winds referred to in the previous chapter.

The Poniente is cooling and humid, with humidity levels which have been registered at up to 95%, whilst the Levante is hot and dry, with humidity levels dropping to around 30%. Anybody who has been in Jerez at the height of summer, with temperatures well above 30°C, and a Levante wind blowing knows what a debilitating climate this can be. A long, hot summer heatwave with an almost constant Levante has been known to drive people crazy!

Put simply, the Poniente has a beneficial effect in the vineyards tempering the heat and creating conditions for a balanced ripening of the grapes. On the other hand, too much Levante has a negative effect, as it slows down phenolic ripening and can create an unbalanced crop of grapes. The specific issue is that the overnight dew which has collected on the leaves and berries, and which is of a beneficial nature to the vine's ripening process, is very quickly burnt away before it can be of use, causing considerable stress to the plant's system.

Evapotranspiration is the process by which water is transferred from the land to the atmosphere by evaporation from the soil and other surfaces, and by transpiration from plants)

On the whole, however, the climate is particularly appropriate for the growing of grapes for Sherry production. Although the summers are dry with high temperatures,

factors which provoke high levels of evapotranspiration, the region's particularly close proximity to the Atlantic helps maintain reasonable levels of humidity and moderates the temperatures somewhat, a fact which is very noticeable at night, and helps to reduce the levels of stress in the vines. In general terms, the average annual temperature is 17.3°C, and even in the coldest months of January and February, the temperatures seldom fall below 6°C, with an average value of around 11°C.

The hottest months are July and August, when it can get as hot as 33°C, but where the average is normally around 25°C. The above temperatures are shade temperatures. In reality, it is a great deal hotter.

Rainfall is usually around 600 litres per square metre each year, with most of it falling in the winter months of December, January and February. Rain is virtually unknown in the months of July and August.

In most years this situation is quite satisfactory for the wellbeing of the Sherry vineyards, one of the most important factors being that the all important nocturnal humidity remains quite high, even during the hottest of summers due to the influence of the Atlantic Ocean and the low lying vineyard locations. Over a full year, the Sherry Triangle sees in excess of 170 days of clear blue skies, somewhere in the region of 70 days of rain and a very high level of sunlight hours per year – at around 3,200.

For the more technically minded:

International Climate Coefficients

Nocturnal Cooling Degree Index	16.9°C
Winkler Coefficient	2,705
Branas Heliothermal Value	11.9
Huglin Index	2,705

Data Source - C.R.D.O. Jerez – Xérès – Sherry

Annual Rainfall from 2004/05 – 2015/16 (litres per square metre)

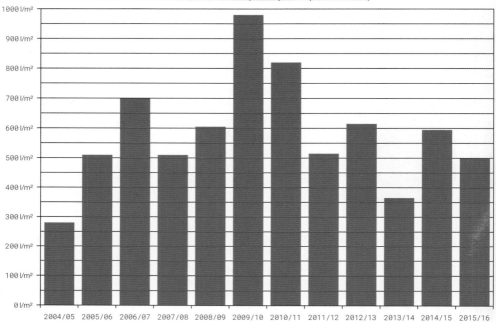

Monthly Rainfall Average from 1986 – 2016 (mm)

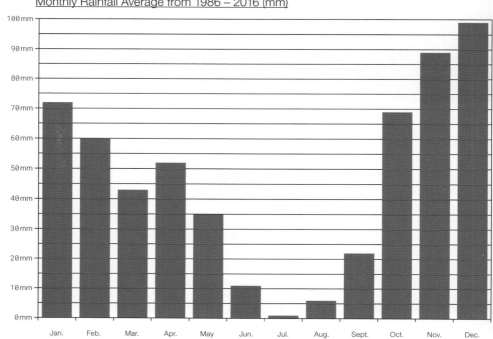

Monthly Temperatures in 2016 (°C)

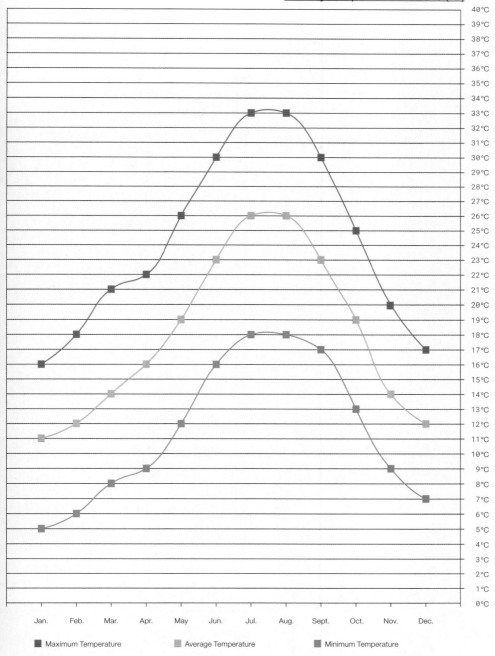

■ Maximum Temperature   ■ Average Temperature   ■ Minimum Temperature

All temperatures are shade readings; the actual direct sun temperatures are considerably higher.

Data Source – Enrique Montero, Jerez Viticulturalist *(All)*

4

Viticulture

Grapes

There are only three grape varieties permitted in the production of Sherry. All of them are white varieties.

The principal grape planted is Palomino, also sometimes known as Palomino Fino, or less commonly Listán. This variety occupies around 98% of the planted vineyard and is responsible for all the basic dry styles of Sherry, from Manzanilla and Fino, though Amontillado and Palo Cortado, and finally Oloroso. Palomino grapes may also be stop fermented to produce the sweet grape must used in the creation of Pale Cream Sherries. Most commonly now, however Pale Creams are sweetened using Rectified Concentrated Must (RCM) which is tasteless, easier to handle, and less expensive.

Ripe Palomino Grapes at Harvest Time

There are two other grapes used for Sherry production, mainly to produce sweetening wines.

Firstly, Moscatel, which in this case is a strain of Muscat of Alexandria, and is known locally as Moscatel de Chipiona, as that is where it principally grows, in the sandy, alluvial soil of that town, and nearby Chiclana.

The final grape is Pedro Ximénez, or PX, which tends to be grown in the heavier clay soils at the bottom of the Albariza slopes, when it is grown in the Marco de Jerez. More usually nowadays however, by special dispensation from the local, Spanish and EU regulatory authorities, it is permitted to bring PX down from the region of Montilla-Moriles in Córdoba Province where it is the dominant grape, and is easier and cheaper to cultivate. It may be brought to Jerez either as fresh or raisined grapes to be processed there, or more usually as young wine; made from grapes which have already been sunned and stop fermented by fortification; and which is now sufficiently mature to be able to enter the Sherry maturation process.

In the relatively normal 2016 vintage, the following volumes of must, with classification granted to create Sherry were produced from the 3 permitted varieties, within the Marco de Jerez.

Production Volumes 2016 Harvest

Palomino	378,715	hectolitres
Moscatel	2,935	hectolitres
Pedro Ximénez	2,700	hectolitres

Data Source - C.R.D.O. Jerez – Xérès – Sherry

In the same harvest some 65,800 hl. of Palomino must were declassified. Most of this would have been used to create light white wines with denomination Vino de la Tierra de Cadiz.

Managing the Vineyard

In excess of 60% of the vineyard is now managed by mechanical means, all the way through from autumn ploughing to the harvest itself, and over the last 20 years or so the planting format, as well as the method of pruning and training have been adapted to allow this increase in mechanisation.

Rather than the traditional Vara y Pulgar (Finger and thumb) method of pruning, over 50% of vines are now trellised on wires in a simple cordon formation purely for reasons of mechanisation. This percentage is likely to increase in the future, as more and more vineyards are managed in this way.

The commercially viable life of a Palomino vine is around 40 years, which theoretically means that some 2 -3 % of the vineyard needs to be replaced every season.

The first step is the selection of the rootstock. Not only does a Phylloxera resistant rootstock need to be chosen, as the scourge of the Phylloxera vastatrix hit the region in the late 19th. Century. It was first detected in Jerez in July 1894. Care must also be taken to select a rootstock which can cope with the high levels of lime and chalk in the soil, and help prevent the onset of chlorosis in the developing plant during its active cycle. Many rootstocks have been used effectively in the past, notably 161-49, 333EM and 41B, but the most popular at present is 13-5 EVEX, not only for its resistance to Phylloxera, to fungal diseases in general, specifically high resistance to chlorosis, but also for its superior compatibility with Palomino Fino, particularly in terms of yield per vine, most especially in years of low rainfall, but also importantly, it encourages the production of grapes with higher total acidity than other commonly used rootstocks.

El Rancho de la Merced

There has been an agricultural and viticultural research station in Jerez since 1943. It was initially set up and run by Gonzalo Fernández de Bobadilla, as part of the Spanish National Institute of Agronomy, but is now part of the Andalucían Government's Research and Development Body for Agriculture and Fisheries. A vast proportion of its work has been done in isolating the best rootstocks suitable for Sherry vineyards with the very specific soil and climate influences of the area, as well as combating the Phylloxera vastatrix louse. A study completed by Viticultural Director Miguel Lara Benitez, and renowned local viticulturist Alberto García de Luján describes how 13-5 EVEX is the most balanced rootstock available, as mentioned in the previous section, in respect of not just Phylloxera and chlorosis control, but also yield, potential alcohol, viable new wood production, root development and drought resistance, suitability for grafting, and when grafted with Palomino scions delivers grapes with higher levels of total acidity than other rootstocks such as 41 –B and 333 EM.

EVEX is the French acronym given by OIV to the Jerez Viticultural Station, and the rootstock is named for them in honour of the years of work which has gone into isolating

Rancho Viticulturalist Miguel Lara in his 13-5 EVEX Nursery

this particular stock. La **E**stación de **V**iticultura **E**spañola de **X**érès. There is a new rootstock in development, with the working name of RM 2 (Rancho Merced 2), but which is yet to be ratified and approved by the OIV. Naturally there are other rootstocks in common use, the most common being 333EM and 41-B which in fact have the highest resistance to chlorosis, but do not have the all round versatility of 13-5.

This combined with work done in clonal selection of Palomino to minimise variations in yield, Baumé and acidity has given Sherry grape growers a major bonus in eliminating both physical and commercial risks in the vineyard. Work is ongoing, with 29 clones in total having been isolated, of which 4 are considered the best and these are currently the subject of further, more detailed research.

The Rancho holds a "Plasma Bank" of both rootstocks and clones, which are sold on to local horticultural nurseries for propagation and sale to grape growers.

Vineyard Tasks

Once a plot of old vines has been grubbed up, it is usual to leave the land fallow, or with only shallow or surface rooted crops planted, to allow the subsoil to rest before replanting with deep rooted vines. In Jerez the very minimum length of time considered appropriate is 3-4 years, but the norm is closer to 7.

Given the poor levels of organic materials and nutrients found in Albariza soils, it is necessary prior to new planting to deeply excavate the plot to be replanted and to add high levels of well composted nutrients. Deep excavation also creates sufficient space for the newly planted rootstock to spread its roots and become sufficiently active and acclimatised to its new environment for the graft to be done successfully and a vigorous plant to be created.

Field grafting is still the norm in Jerez, although some of the bigger vineyard owners are gradually moving towards bench grafted nursery sourced plants using their preferred rootstock, but with scion material taken from their own actively growing vines.

Planting is now normally done in rows running down the 10 – 15% slopes and in a north to south direction to give the best light exposure. In order to accommodate mechanised work, vines are now planted in rows 2.30 metres apart with the distance between plants 1.15 metres. This rectangular plotting also creates sufficient competition between plants to give balanced yields.

When any vineyard area has been replanted, the yield of grapes it can produce for inclusion in Sherry production is carefully controlled by the Consejo Regulador as follows:

Year 1	0	kg/ha
Year 2	2,857	kg/ha
Year 3	5,714	kg/ha
Year 4	8,571	kg/ha

After which it can produce the maximum permitted yield.

Tractors can then work up and down the rows without creating ridges in the soil which might be conducive to disease in the early years after planting, by exposing the graft point to air.

Given the nature of the planting system, the annual rainfall, the vineyard inclination and the soil type, one of the most important tasks of the year is the "Aserpia". This is done in early autumn, almost immediately following the harvest and before the main winter rains, and it requires the creation a series of troughs or gullies down each row of vines and between each plant in every row. These troughs will now hold the winter rains to feed each and every plant. Without them most of the rain would simply flow down the slopes to the bottom of the field!

As can be seen from the photographs to the left, this task is also now carried out mechanically in many vineyards. It is a particularly labour intensive and costly task to undertake manually.

The winter thinning and pruning operation is also carried out at about this time, but will vary by vineyard site. The important thing is that it is carried out before the heavy winter rains, so that the surface is clear and not compacted once the rains arrive, to allow maximum penetration. The definitive growth cycle pruning is done in early winter, traditionally starting in mid-December well before the first buds begin to appear to generate the fruiting growth for the coming season, and to allow the new growth to be trained in Cordon fashion onto the permanent wire structures now in place.

Albariza soils are particularly notable for their deficiency in natural organic material, so it is vital to ensure that levels of nitrogen, phosphorous and potassium are balanced and corrected when and where necessary. It is common practice to allow the fallen autumn leaves to decompose into the soil to increase its organic structure.

Vineyard Pests and Diseases

The principal vineyard pest in the Sherry vineyards, as it is in most European vineyards is Lobesia botrana, or European vineyard moth. This moth is of the Tortricidae family, which also contains the codling moth, the wrecker of many an apple orchard. In the last 20 years controls have been refined using techniques of sexual confusion in young males by setting female pheromone traps, with considerable success, and although the process is extremely labour intensive and requires consistent monitoring, It is a particularly non-invasive procedure.

Most diseases are of a fungal nature, the principal ones being oidium (powdery mildew), downy mildew and botrytis. These are of special concern if rain falls early into the hot summer months, and are in the main treated with commercial systemic fungicides such as cuprosan or propineb.

The Prime Albariza Vineyard of
Macharnudo Alto

5

The Production
Process

Harvest

The harvest of Palomino begins with the grapes in those vineyards furthest from the sea, with the warmest climates, and naturally therefore where the grapes ripen earliest. The minimum legal parameter for potential alcohol is 10.5° Baumé, but the norm is almost always closer to 11.5° or 12°, with some musts reaching 13.5°. Grapes will normally be over-ripe, but not too ripe; will be golden in colour and with no signs of raisining.

Maximum production is 11,428 kilos per hectare, for wines to be produced with protected denomination Jerez-Xérès-Sherry or Manzanilla de Sanlúcar de Barrameda. Total permitted yields are 14,285 kilos per hectare, with the extra 2,857 kilos being declassified to other uses. However if total yields exceed 14,285 kilos then the entire production is declassified.

Two vital measurements are the level of polyphenols and of gluconic acid. The former evolves from skin, pip and stem contact, and the latter is a compound found in very over-ripe grapes (botrytis). High contents of either would at a later stage inhibit the potential for Flor to develop fully and evenly.

The target values for the base wine to be produced are as follows:

Alcohol	12	%
Total Acidity (in tartaric)	5	g/l
Dry Extract	22 – 25	g/l
pH	3.3	
Glycerine	7.0 – 7.5	g/l

As previously mentioned, in excess of 60% of grapes are now machine harvested, often at night, and most certainly in the coolest parts of the day.

Due mainly to climate change factors, harvests in recent years have started increasingly earlier. In 2015 the first grapes were harvested on 3rd. August and by 4th. September there was very little left to be picked. Forty years ago, this would have been the approximate start date. It is, of course possible that in training the vines on wires, and lifting the bunches further from the floor to facilitate machine harvesting, the grapes themselves stay warmer at night during the final stages of ripening, due to lower levels of night-time dew forming on their skins, and so evolve their sugars more rapidly. This theory is countered by some of the more traditional growers who still prune Vara y Pulgar, who say that their grapes are ripening earlier too.

Pressing and Fermentation

Pressing

There are 28 separate Press Houses in the Sherry Production area, 14 of them within the municipal boundaries of Jerez, 5 in Sanlúcar and the remaining 9 in other municipal locations. They are known in Spanish as Bodegas de Elaboración or Lagares, and between them crushed some 57 million kilos of grapes in the 2016 harvest, a relatively modest total when compared to the 76 million kilos crushed in 2015. They are either owned by the bigger shipping Bodegas, for example, Barbadillo, González Byass and Grupo Estévez, otherwise they are Co-operatives or independently owned.

The grapes, either handpicked of machine harvested, are brought to the press house facilities. Almost invariably now these are located in the vineyards or in purpose built facilities on the outskirts of one of the three towns. Hand picked grapes will need to be destalked, and machine harvested grapes will, in the main, already be stalk-free.

The machine harvested grapes will give producers an early selection of juices which will eventually become Finos. In the bottom of the trailer there will be around 20% of the grapes' weight already in juice form. This will be drawn off first and kept separate, to be fermented separately in many cases. It will be naturally low in polyphenols, having had no stalk contact, and little or no skin and pip contact. This is locally known as the "escurrido".

The Photograph above to the left shows its decantation by gravity from the grape collection truck at the La Gitana "EL Cuadrado" vineyard.

The rest of the grapes, whether machine or hand picked will be dropped into a long V shaped hopper, with an Archimedean screw at its base. Once the hopper is full, the screw will start to rotate, and via a series of slotted conveyor belts the grapes will be lifted and dropped into the top of a rotating drum sieve, from which the "free run juice" or first pressing will be drawn. This is known as the "Primera Yema", and, including the "escurrido" will account for between 60 and 75% of the grapes' potential juice in volume.

This is the part of the production which will be most suitable for biological ageing. The final fraction of juice is then pressed out of the grape pulp, to be used almost exclusively for Oloroso production.

Some bodegas, such as Barbadillo and Hidalgo La Gitana, whose production is principally Manzanilla Fina, will blend the escurrido with the Primera Yema. Others, such as González Byass, whose production is almost entirely of biologically aged Sherries, but of differing levels of complexity, will keep the Primera Yema and the escurrido separate in the fermentation phase. It must be stressed that the percentages used above are guidelines only. Each and every Bodega has its own style requirements which are entirely dependent on their commercial portfolio of Sherries. Some, naturally, will use some of the Primera Yema, or even the Escurrido to produce oxidatively aged Sherries, but they will show greater finesse than those from the final pressing, and as a consequence be directed towards a higher quality, more refined finished product. A good example of this is the relatively new Harveys range, in which the four dry styles made from Palomino are all Primera Yema wines.

The next, and absolutely vital phase is to clean the must prior to fermentation. The vineyard is hot and the air thick with dust blown up from the Albariza soils onto the grape skins, and all the materials used in the harvest. The juice is at this stage a fairly unpleasant looking shade of brownish grey, and if it were not cleaned up fermentation would most certainly be compromised.

There are 2 principal ways of cleaning the must. The first is a static decantation in a chilled tank, at around 16°C for around 18 hours to precipitate most of the solids and then centrifuging the cleaner juice to remove smaller particles. Barbadillo use this method at their Gibalbín pressing and fermentation facility.

The second is to pump inert gas, such as nitrogen into the bottom of the holding tank, and force the solid particles to rise to the top of the tank, leaving the bright juice below.

This is then drained out from the bottom of the tank, lightly dosed with SO_2 before being sent to ferment. This more modern method was pioneered by González Byass. The lovely, technical, Spanish word for this clarification process is "desfangado" – literally translated as de-mudding!

Maximum production is 70 litres per 100 kilos of grapes.

The pH level at this stage is vital, since at very specific levels it protects the juice from bacterial contamination during the alcoholic fermentation. It rises during the final phase of ripening of Palomino to a value sometimes close to 3.9 or 4.0 and its downward correction is essential. Nowadays this is mainly done by the addition of tartaric acid prior to fermentation, but still occasionally gypsum is added in the older, more traditional manner.

Fermentation

Once the must is clean and chemically balanced, the alcoholic fermentation can begin. Most wineries now use commercially selected yeasts, to ensure a balanced and thorough conversion of the sugars in the juice to alcohol. It is mainly done in stainless steel tanks at a controlled temperature of around 23-24°C. This may seem high for a white wine, but is appropriate in Sherry production, as the primary aromas of the grapes are effectively unimportant in the finished wine.

There is still a small amount of barrel fermentation carried out. One notable example of this is in the Estévez Group of companies, where the base wine for the Valdespino Fino Inocente Solera and its follow-on Tio Diego Amontillado Solera is barrel fermented, albeit within the cool conditions of the modern winery on the outskirts of Jerez.

The butts used are the same ones every year, meticulously cleaned before use, and are used for storing young wine following harvest until they are needed again for fermentation purposes. As they are well seasoned they are virtually free of any tannin residues, which would inhibit Flor growth if imparted to the fermenting must.

As previously indicated, different quality batches with specific style tendencies already apparent will all be fermented separately, although homogenised into groups with particularly similar analyses, to create large batch fermentations. As with all wines, the fermentation process will be very carefully monitored by oenologists, to ensure that the conversion of sugars into alcohol is progressing normally, but also to check that all the other enzymatic processes are proceeding correctly.

There are several by products which are created during fermentation which will be absolutely critical in the evolution of the base wine into mature Sherry.

These are:

Glycerol, acetaldehyde, certain acids such as succinic and lactic, as well as aromatic compounds and higher alcohols.

Modern Fermentation Tanks

The tumultuous stage of fermentation, in which the majority of sugars are converted, lasts about a week, and over the following 2 weeks or so, all the remaining sugars will have been converted and this part of the process is complete, with the young wine now at a minimum of 10.5% alcohol, but more normally closer to 12%..

The young wine is still called "mosto" or "must" in Sherry production, as theoretically it is not yet "wine", as it has not yet been fortified. There is a very pleasant custom of selling some of this mosto to the local bars and taverns, where it is sold during the autumn and winter months, as a very pleasant aperitif, or young wine to accompany the autumnal and winter regional cuisine, often rabbit and hare or small seasonal game birds.

That part which is destined to become Sherry – the majority, will now need to be cleaned and the solid residues from fermentation removed. The young wine is transferred from the tanks in which it fermented into holding tanks where, over the next month or so, it will undergo static decantation, either lightly chilled or at ambient winter temperatures. If done carefully, this decantation of the lees to the bottom of the tank will add another layer of complexity to the wine.

First Classification and Fortification

Detailed records of the origins and potential style of each fermentation batch will now be checked, and the base wine will be analysed and tasted to decide on its future course. At this stage it is, in the main, simply separated out as wine suitable for biological ageing, to produce Finos and their derivatives, or for physio-chemical ageing to produce Olorosos.

The analyses will be showing the tendencies, but it is now up to the winemakers and tasters to take the definitive decision. Fino translates as fine or delicate, whereas Oloroso translates as pungent or smelly. Tasting of Sherry at this and most other stages of the wine's evolution is done almost entirely on the nose, and a decision will be taken for each batch, be it a barrel, a vat or a tank.

The taking of these samples from barrel is done by means of a venencia. This is a tool used specifically in the Sherry region for this purpose, and unique to it.

Venencia has its origins in the Spanish verb "Avenenciar" – meaning "To come to an agreement". In the 18th. and 19th Centuries, most shipping houses did not have as much stock as is currently the case, and often needed to purchase finished wine for a shipping blend, or to top up their stocks, from an Almacenista. The venencia was developed to allow samples to be taken from the top bung hole of the butts on offer to be nosed by the prospective purchaser. The venencia comprises an 8cm long cylindrical cup, around 3cm in diameter and attached to a long, flexible handle along one side. It is plunged into the butt, to around a middle level, and sherry withdrawn.

Sampling the New Wine

As can be seen in the photograph on the next page, it is then poured, from a height into the tasting glass, which causes all the aromas of the wine to be released to great effect, and the wine nosed by as many people as are present. It has become such a polished technique, that there is now an annual competition during Harvest Festival to find the best Venenciador in the area. The flexibility of the handle makes them devilishly difficult to use, and the amateur attempting the procedure for the first time will finish with more sherry on his sleeve or on the floor than in the glass. The handles of old venencias used to be made from whale "whiskers", but unsurprisingly that is no longer the case and high grade flexible plastic with a diameter of about 7mm is used.

In Sanlúcar de Barrameda the device used is called a Caña, and is shaped from a length of bamboo cane, with the bottom section left in the full round to create a cup, and the rest of the length cut to around 2cm wide to form the handle. The reason for using a lighter weight device is to create a lower level of disturbance in the Flor layer through which it passes to collect the sample. This implement can also be seen in use on the next page.

The most delicate wines, the Finos destined to age under Flor will be fortified to 15 or 15.5 % alcohol, the optimum alcohol levels at which Flor will grow, and the Olorosos will

Using a Jerez Venencia

be fortified to 17% at which level Flor cannot survive. There is a classic local adage – "If in doubt, don't". In other words if there is the slightest doubt or worry, err on the side of Fino. Once the alcohol has been increased to 17%, that deed cannot be undone!

The finest, at this first classification stage will be designated as Raya (/), the next, where doubt may be occurring Raya y Punto (/.) and the fullest in body Dos Rayas (//).

The liquid used to make this fortification is a 50/50 blend of the wine itself, and pure wine alcohol, distilled to 95% alcohol by volume, the final blend of which has an alcoholic strength of around 54%. It is known locally as "mitad y mitad" – or half and half.

Those wines destined to age in Olorosos Soleras are now known as Oloroso vintage, and the Finos are called Sobretablas. The word Sobretablas derives from the times when the wine would have gone straight into barrel to start ageing. The wine would then have been "Sobre" – Lying on "Tablas" – Staves, rather that Sobre Lías – on its lees.

Current practice for Finos is to hold the wine in tank until the spring, when a second classification is done, simply to confirm exactly which batches are suitable for biological ageing and to eliminate those which have not retained their delicacy over the winter months.

Using a Sanlúcar Caña

Second Classification and Fortification

This second classification will now finally decide which of the Sherries that have up to now only been fortified to 15 – 15.5%, those initially classified as Raya (/) or Raya y punto (/.) all of which could eventually be made into Fino, actually will be.

The very finest will now be identified as Palma ⨍ those not quite so fine as Palma y punto ⨍., as potentially a Fino, perhaps not so delicate, and maybe veering towards a potential Amontillado. Those which have lost a considerable level of delicacy, but which are still elegant will be marked as Palo Cortado ⨍. All these wines will be closely monitored, their alcohol levels left unchanged, and a decision eventually made as to how long to keep the latter two in biological ageing.

All of the above symbols are references to times past, when the wine at this stage of development would have been stored in butts, and these were the chalk mark identification symbols which would have been written on the butt ends by the taster to identify the style characteristics of each one. Nowadays the references are kept in computer records, but the traditional terminology is still used verbally. These wines are still in the phase known as Sobretablas, prior to entering the appropriate Solera system. They are still vintage wines and may be stored in butt, in vat or in larger tanks.

In early Spring, or even earlier, a veil, or thin film of white solid mass will spontaneously start to appear on the surface of all those wines which have alcohol levels of 15 – 15.5%. This is Flor. It is a veil of yeasts which will now allow these wines to develop in a process of biological, non-oxidative ageing, which is very specific to Sherry.

The conditions for its growth are that all the fermentable sugar in the wine should have been used up, the surface of the wine should be in direct contact with air, ambient temperature should be between 16°C and 20°C, levels of polyphenols at around 200mg/l (expressed in gallic acid), volatile acidity no higher than 0.35 g/l in acetic acid, and levels of gluconic acid lower than 400 mg/l. Flor has a particular dislike for tannin, so any butts used for storing this young Sobretablas Fino must be very well seasoned.

Sherry Barrels

A Sherry barrel is known as a Butt, a "Bota" in Spanish, and has a nominal capacity of 500 litres. Nominal, because there are few around of this size these days. They used to be used to ship Sherry, but as most Sherry is sold already bottled, or in bulk containers, there are not many still in use. However, the word is still used by the regulatory authorities as a measure of stocks in Bodegas or of the quantity produced in the harvest. Most butts used in Solera systems have a larger capacity of around 566 or 600 litres.

Confusingly perhaps these are expressed locally in terms of the number of Bodega jugs – "Arrobas" which each can hold. An Arroba, pictured amongst the traditional equipment on p.66 has a capacity of 16.66 litres.

It must be mentioned here that Flor will have started to develop and be visible on the surface of all the young wines, just after the end of the alcoholic fermentation. Its effect however will have been minimal. In Jerez it would have died off during the colder winter weather, and will have played virtually no role in the biological ageing process. In El Puerto and Sanlúcar, where it would have grown a little more thickly, and here a major percentage of the wine eventually ages biologically, so its minor effect would have been, if anything, beneficial.

Flor – An Explanation.

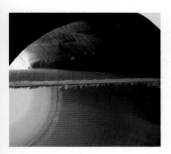

Other wine regions around the world have wines which develop in contact with yeasts, notably in Condado de Huelva and Rueda in Spain, as well as Jura in France and Tokaji in Hungary, but the complexity which the yeast strains which have been isolated in the Sherry region create in its wine is unique.

For decades it has been written and argued that there are 4 separate yeasts which make up the film of Flor, some being more prevalent in the early stages of biological ageing, and some more prominent in the later phases.

They are classified as:
Saccharomyces Beticus
Saccharomyces Cheresiensis
Saccharomyces Montuliensis
Saccharomyces Rouxii

Recent microbiological research has now proposed that Sacch. beticus, Sacch. cheresiensis and Sacch. rouxii are in fact just synonyms for Sacch. cerevisiae. However, there are many eminent microbiologists, working either in the Sherry industry, or in pure microbiological research who insist that the four Flor yeasts are not synonyms for, but in fact four separate races of Sacch. Cerevisiae, which have slightly different attributes. In fact, it has been definitively shown that Sacch. montuliensis and Sacch. rouxii consume the most ethanol, create greater quantities of acetaldehyde and can survive in higher levels of alcohol than Sacch. beticus. For this reason, whereas in all three towns Sacch. beticus is the dominant race, Sacch. montuliensis and Sacch. rouxii are found in greater proportions in Jerez itself, with Sacch. montuliensis often barely detectable in the Soleras of Sanlúcar. A significant contributory factor in the aroma and palate profiles of Manzanilla Fina as compared to Jerez Fino.

The genetic microbiology debate will no doubt continue, but what is certain is that the physiological properties of the yeast film, in metabolising ethanol to ethanal (acetaldehyde), reducing acetic acid levels and consuming glycerine; combined with the autolytic properties created by the continually dying yeast cells, delivers in biologically aged Sherries one of the most complex sets of aroma and flavour compounds in the world of white wine making.

The yeast strains have their origins in the complex microflora which develops quite spontaneously on the skin of the grapes in the vineyard, and which remain submerged in the juice of the grape into and through the fermentation. They are also present in the air itself, circulating in the Bodegas.

Sacch. beticus is the most important component of Flor in all three Sherry towns, but then in Jerez and to a lesser extent in El Puerto, Sacch. montuliensis is the nexrt most important, but as described above it is often not a significant element of Flor make up in Sanlúcar, where Sacch. cheriensis is often more vigorous. They also vary in proportion from Bodega to Bodega, which could go part way to explaining why, say a Fino from one bodega in El Puerto can taste so very different from a Fino produced in a Bodega in another part of town. No matter what the correct microbiological position is, this phenomenon is what gives us Fino and Manzanilla, as well as eventually Amontillado and Palo Cortado!

Flor needs certain physical requirements to survive, and being yeast it also requires nutrients. Firstly the alcohol level needs to be a maximum of 16% by volume, above which level it struggles to survive, although it has in fact been observed growing on wines with alcohol values of 17 or 17.5% The temperature in the Bodega needs to be in the range of 16°C – 20°C, the humidity needs to be around 65% and those values need to remain as constant as possible.

The Sherry Bodegas have been constructed over the centuries to reflect those needs, with thick, high walls, with

high level, small windows, fitted with blinds, and where possible oriented towards south west, in order to pick up the beneficial cooling and dampening effects of the Poniente wind.

These temperature and humidity factors also go part way to explaining why Flor grows more thickly, and for a longer period of the year in the two coastal towns of El Puerto and Sanlúcar, where it is more humid and where the temperature varies less than it does in inland Jerez. The primary nutrient the Flor picks up is the carbon molecules of the ethanol. This is the kick starter, but after that the other primary nutrient is the glycerol which was created during the fermentation process.

The third vital nutrient of course, as it is for all aerobic yeasts, is oxygen. The butts which make up the Fino Soleras are only filled to about 85% capacity to allow the Flor to breathe, and in addition are only loosely bunged, to allow air to circulate a little in the surface area above the wine, inside the butt. The film of Flor yeast, as well as acting as a barrier to oxygen, and preventing discolouration though oxidation has a multiple effect in creating and developing the flavours of Fino as it ages. From a biochemistry point of view the Flor yeasts metabolise some of the hydrocarbon components of the wine, and there is a notable reduction in levels of organic and amino acids, ethanol, glycerine and acetic acid, to the point where these latter two elements virtually disappear.

The reduction of glycerine is fundamental here. It is an element which gives a perception of sweetness, and its effective elimination from a mature Fino underlines its dryness to a remarkable degree. This extreme dryness accentuates the sensation of savouriness created by the increased level of acetaldehyde, often referred to as salinity in the palate, which balances the relatively low level of acidity, and because the volatile acidity is also reduced to almost zero, we are left with elegant, delicately bitter flavours which produce a remarkably long finish.

In addition, as the yeast cells reproduce and die, the dead yeast cells fall through the wine and as they decompose their make up of amino-acids, enzymes and mannoproteins not only create nutrients for new yeast populations, but also give Fino Sherry a distinctly autolytic aroma and flavour. Interestingly, recent research has shown that the mannoproteins produced can also help the wine's natural tartrate stability making a pre-bottling refrigeration less necessary. This fact also aides the longevity and stability in bottle of "En Rama" Manzanillas and Finos. Naturally, the more scales there are in a Fino Solera, the more times the barrels are refreshed, the more these dead and dying yeast cells are disturbed, albeit very gently, the greater this autolytic effect will be.

This complex and unique set of factors combine to give Fino its decidedly almondy characteristics on both the nose and the palate, and the more mature the Fino, the more pronounced these aromas and flavours become. Combined with the manifold increase in acetaldehyde created by the biological ageing process, we can see why, in pure tasting terms, by the time a mature Fino is bottled, both the primary and secondary aromas and flavours have all but disappeared.

Self-evidently, if Fino is taken from the younger nurseries of the Solera to be bottled as a less mature less expensive wine, some traces of these primary or secondary elements will still be apparent.

Classic Sherry Bodega Architecture

Sherry Ageing

The Solera Systems

The Solera system imprints a very special dynamic on the ageing process, and influences the character of the wines produced in a singular way. In principle it retains the style and quality of the wine within the Solera, whilst eliminating vintage variation from one year to another.

A Solera is, in essence a series of tiers of the same wine, but at gradually increasing levels of average age and complexity. It is often depicted graphically as a series of levels of butts stacked on top of each other, with the youngest at the top and the oldest at the bottom. This is not necessarily always the case, although it is a relatively simple graphic with which to gain an understanding of the mechanics of the process.

In actuality, many Bodegas prefer to keep each of the tier levels together in one specific building or part of a building for reasons either of ease of movement or especially in the case of Fino and Manzanilla for reasons of temperature and humidity. In many traditional bodegas, especially in Jerez itself, it is not uncommon for Finos to be kept at ground level, where it is cooler and more humid, with maybe fuller bodied wines, Amontillados, Palo Cortados and Olorosos in the tiers above, where the air is marginally warmer.

There are indeed bodegas where Solera wines are at ground level, with their 1st. 2nd and 3rd. Criaderas stacked above them. There are no hard and fast rules, but, whatever the case, the wines do not, in any way, flow directly down through the tiers.

Taking wine out of the butts is known locally as a "Saca".

Refreshing the older butts with younger wine is called "Rocío" – literally sprinkling. In all cases the wines extracted at any one saca from any one scale are blended together for the sake of homogeneity and then added in equal proportions to the receiving butts in the next scale.

In the first photograph on the previous page the third scale (or clase) of the Solear Manzanilla Solera system can be seen at Bodegas Barbadillo in Sanlúcar de Barrameda. Note that the numbers and arrows on the front of the end butt indicate that it is one of 1050 butts containing Solear at the same stage of its evolution, and that all the barrels, in the bottom, the middle and the top rows are of the same wine. This particular building in the Barbadillo complex has been found to have exactly the right natural temperature and levels of humidity to mature the wine at this specific stage of its evolution.

In the other photograph can be seen three scales of the La Ina Fino Solera at Lustau, where the Solera itself is at ground level, the 1st. Criadera in the row above it, and the 2nd. Criadera in the row above that. They are not physically interconnected in any way. They are however permanent fixtures and are never moved, unless one of them needs repair work done on it. Some solera systems have been in place for over a hundred years.

For each style of wine held by any Bodega, there will be a Solera system. The oldest wine in that system will be contained in butts also known as the Solera. There can be any number of butts in this Solera, from as few as 8 or 10 in the case of a particularly venerable or special wine, to many thousands for a big branded commercial wine. The Solera for Williams & Humbert's Dry Sack brand, for example, has 16.024 butts.

Next come the Nurseries, or Criaderas, which are numbered consecutively from 1st. Criadera which is the oldest, through 2nd, 3rd, 4th and so on, up to as many as the Bodega needs to create the complexity of that particular Sherry. The greater number of Criaderas, the more complex the wine in the Solera will be. These Criaderas are commonly called the "scales", and the whole process referred to as "running the scales"

The process of managing a Solera system is relatively simple, but seems particularly complicated at first sight. When sherry is needed from any scale in the system, for blending purposes, a calculation is made from the quantity of litres required in total as to which butts that sherry will be drawn from. The calculation is quite simply based on the quantity to be taken from each butt, at a percentage never more than 20% or 30% of its contents in any one year, and an identification of those butts in that scale which have least recently been accessed.

If, for example 10,000 litres are needed, somewhere around 65 litres will be drawn from the 150 least recently used butts in that scale.

Then, the same number of butts will be accessed from the next youngest Criadera scale, and the same amount of sherry take from each of them. This wine will then be blended together and used to refill the space left in the older Criadera. During the next 3 to 6 months or so, the younger wine added will take on the complexities and characteristics of the older wine, and after that time, the quality and complexity will have totally homogenised and the whole process can start again.

Classic Scale Running
Above & Opposite

It must be emphasised that the mathematics described above are entirely theoretical in order to create a working example. Many Bodegas run the scales more often, taking out less wine at a time, and vice versa. There are no fixed rules or formulae; each and every Bodega has its own rulebook, and as long as it adheres to the maximum rotation regulations of the Consejo Regulador, and the House style remains consistent for marketing purposes, that is fine.

Mechanized Scale Running

6

Sherry Styles

The Many Styles of Sherry

It is important to recognise that the process of running the scales of a Solera varies in each of the categories of Sherry produced, as the ageing mechanics are different for Fino, Amontillado, Palo Cortado and Oloroso.

Fino and Manzanilla Soleras

Whilst the principal objective in all solera systems is to maintain a homogenous house style for the Sherry in question, there are particular, specific requirements in managing a Fino solera.

Put quite simply, a Fino Solera system is dependent on Flor, and Flor's survival is dependent on the Solera system. As young Fino enters the youngest Criadera scale of a Solera system from its vintage – Sobretablas phase, it will be rich in nutrients to feed the Flor – Glycerine, Ethanol, organic and amino acids, including acetic acid. The Flor on the youngest Criadera will be the thickest. As each stage of the Solera is gradually refreshed, nutrients are passed down scale by scale, each time offering nutrient levels to the older wine it refreshes, but naturally at each scale stage, less and less of these nutrients will be available, and on the Fino Solera itself, the film of Flor will have become relatively thin. It will still be thick enough however to prevent the wine in the butts from oxidising.

Flor is not a static organism. Yeast cells are constantly dying, and new seeding cells from the atmosphere take their place. As they die, and decompose, dropping to the bottom of the butt, many compounds are created, one such being mannoproteins. These too become a source of nutrition to the new yeast cells, but also as the cells decompose there is a process of autolysis taking place. This, as in all autolysed wines, becomes a crucial part of the aroma and flavour profile.

In a Fino Solera, it is more usual to take a smaller amount of wine at each Saca, and to do it more often. This has a double advantage in that it more regularly enhances the nutrient levels for the Flor, thus keeping it growing more thickly and preventing oxidation. It also means that Fino is being taken out more frequently for blending and bottling, so that it reaches the market in a fresher condition.

At González Byass for example, the Tio Pepe Solera system has 4 levels, the Solera itself and 3 criaderas.
25% is removed from each level in any one year, but in 4 separate sacas to keep the Flor as well nourished as possible, and as often as possible. It can therefore be said that Tio Pepe, at the moment of bottling has an average age of 4 years.

When a Fino butt is being refreshed, it is important that the veil of Flor is disturbed as little as possible. To that end various devices have been devised over time to ensure that the wine is taken out carefully, and that the new wine added does so at a level below the Flor. Some of these are illustrated on these pages.

All the sacas and rocíos are carried out through the bung hole on the top of the butt. The bung at the bottom of the butt is never removed during the normal course of ageing.

In the case of Fino, even though great care is taken not to disturb the Flor or the dead cells in the bottom of the butt, some agitation necessarily occurs. This too will increase albeit lightly, the incidence of autolytic aromas and flavours in the finished wine. In addition, it must be pointed out that not all Fino goes though the Solera system to the very end. Young Finos may be taken out of the system, for example at the 2nd. Criadera stage and prepared for bottling. These young Finos are lighter, have spent less time in the bodega, have accrued less capital value, and can therefore be sold at a more competitive price. These are the entry point Finos of the multiple retailers. Good entry point wines, but without the complexities and nuances of fully mature Finos, which are necessarily more expensive at the point of sale.

The analytical evolution of a typical Fino Solera can be seen in Table 2 below. Note the early reduction of the alcohol level in the first stage, notwithstanding any evaporation, which in theory would increase the alcohol level, as the Flor feeds on and metabolises the ethanol. Subsequent reductions which take place are also a direct consequence of Flor activity.

Data Source – B. Domecq Williams
– Sherry Uncovered

Table 2

Fino Development

	Average Age, Years.	Alcohol %	Total Acidity g/l	Volatile Acidity g/l
Bas Wine		12.0	5.0	0.40
Sobretabla	0-1	15.5	4.8	0.30
Criadera	1-2	15.3	4.2	0.25
Criadera	2-3	15.2	4.0	0.20
Criadera	3-4	15.0	3.9	0.15
Solera	4-5	14.9	3.8	0.10

Manzanilla

It is important to note the subtle, but vital differences between the evolution of Fino Soleras in Jerez, and to an extent in El Puerto de Santa María to those of Manzanilla Fina Soleras in Sanlúcar de Barrameda.

There is a strange anomaly to note. One of the principal products created by the metabolisation of Flor is acetaldehyde. We also know from physical observation that Flor grows more thickly in Sanlúcar than it does in Jerez. It would therefore be logical to assume that a mature Manzanilla Fina would contain higher levels of acetaldehyde than its Jerez matured counterpart.

However, analysis has shown that in two Soleras, one of Jerez Fino, the other of Manzanilla Fina, both starting with natural levels of acetaldehyde from fermentation of around 100 mg/l, and both having 3 Criaderas and a Solera, the acetaldehyde level in the Jerez Fino at all Solera nursery levels was some 20% higher than that of the Manzanilla Fina. In addition the Solera levels of i-amyl alcohols in the Jerez Fino were around 22% higher than those in Sanlúcar. Those levels in Jerez had increased from the youngest "Sobretablas" stage, whereas those in Sanlúcar had actually decreased.

Acetaldehyde mg/l	Ethyl Acetate mg/l	Glycerine g/l	Dry Exract	Colour 470nm	Gallic Acid mg/l
50	75	7.3	23	0.120	3.1
125	72	3.5	20	0.112	5.3
210	70	1.5	17	0.120	6.8
275	47	0.7	15	0.121	8.2
345	44	0.5	13	0.122	9.6
400	30	0.2	12	0.125	11.0

These factors are part of the reason why Manzanilla smells and tastes much lighter, but at the same time has more zest and bite than its Jerez counterpart. The reasons why these apparent anomalies occur could be many and varied, from increased concentration through water evaporation in the hotter environment of Jerez, through to different population percentages of the four Flor yeast components in the two towns' climatic environments. This latter proposition is by far the more likely, given the much lower levels of Sacch. montuliensis found in Sanlúcar Flor, as described earlier.

It could in some way help to explain why Manzanilla is sometimes referred to as salty or saline, whereas in fact what is being tasted is less aggression stemming from the relatively lower concentrations of these two complex and assertive compounds.

Whatever the reasons, the influence of sodium chloride – sea salt, is not one of them!

To test this assertion I arranged for two samples, one of Manzanilla Fina and the other of Jerez Fino to be analysed for sodium chloride levels by the U.K. Industry's most respected laboratory, Campden BRI. Both wines were from the same Sherry Shipper, of very similar average age and sold in the same U.K. retailer for the same price. Sodium chloride was detected in both wines, with the Manzanilla at 17 mg/l and the Jerez Fino at 12 mg/l. Given all the other flavour elements in both wines, acetaldehyde, autolysis etc.

I would contend that the sodium chloride is close to being undetectable on the palate. In addition, sodium chloride has no aroma!

Sanlúcar in fact has a rather more estuarial river climate than a maritime one, unlike those of the two coastal towns of Rota and Chipiona, and the level of salt in the Guadalquivir is many times lower than that in the sea into which it flows.

Added to this fact, ecological research has shown that aerosols of salt laden water blown in from the sea can travel a maximum of 20 to 30 metres on a normal wind, and a little less than 100 metres in a gale; therefore the chance of either the grapes of the area or the wines being matured in butts behind thick walls being influenced by salt is virtually nil.

What I would suggest is being noticed on the palate is a slightly greater level of primary and secondary flavours which have less competition from the assertive palate influences of acetaldehyde and i-amyl alcohols. Perhaps we would be better served to describe Manzanillas as savoury rather than saline!

Typically a Manzanilla Fina Solera will have more nurseries than a Jerez Fino Solera. Given that the Flor grows more thickly and for a longer part of the year, it needs more nutrient replenishment to do this. Where a Jerez Fino Solera will typically have between 4 and 6 Criaderas, this number can rise to as many as 10 or more in Sanlúcar. They will be refreshed more often, but with lower percentages of wine being taken out and replenished at each saca and rocío. Most of the Sanlúcar Bodegas strive to keep their Flor active throughout the year, and constant nutrient refreshment is vital to achieving this.

The River Guadalquivir at Sanlúcar
Opposite

The next phases

Not all Fino is taken from the Solera systems to be bottled, or to refresh the next scale. It is also removed to refresh the Amontillado Soleras, and in the case of Manzanilla the Manzanilla Pasada Soleras.

Manzanilla Pasada

Most Manzanilla producers will make a Manzanilla Pasada, which is a halfway house style between Fino and Amontillado. It is generally produced in relatively small quantities. They are most often, as in the case of Barbadillo refreshed from a selection of their Manzanilla Fina "Solear" Solera with the Flor eliminated by a light addition of alcohol up to 17%.

There are only a few butts in this particular system, and only around 4.000 half bottles are released every year, and labelled as Manzanilla en Rama denoting that it has been bottled almost directly from the barrel, with minimal intervention. Hidalgo-La Gitana has a similar product known as Manzanilla Pasada Pastrana, after their vineyard of the same name, and again in very limited quantities, also en Rama. Both these Bodegas will use the Pasada Solera to refresh their very small Amontillado soleras.

The word Pasada is only used in descriptions of lightly oxidised Sherries in Sanlúcar. In both Jerez and El Puerto these wines used to be known as Fino-Amontillado, denoting Fino on its way to Amontillado, but still not as complex as a true Amontillado. This terminology may no longer be used in Sherry labelling, with the sole exception of Bodegas Osborne in El Puerto which has been given special dispensation for its Coquinero brand.

Amontillado Soleras

The Sherries which enter an Amontillado Solera will vary immensely, and the way they are managed will necessarily be dependent on the styles and complexities of Amontillados which the Bodega takes to market. Most Bodegas will, in fact have several, separate Amontillado Soleras, the younger ones feeding into the older ones over time.

The simplest, most commercial type of Amontillado Solera will be fed by a Fino probably from only the second or third level on from its Sobretablas stage. The Flor will be killed off by the addition of an alcohol and wine mixture to bring the actual alcohol level to about 17% and added to the space created by a Saca from the youngest Criadera of the Amontillado Solera. This saca will have refreshed the next level down, and so on to the level where Amontillado will have been taken out for bottling, or for feeding the youngest nursery of an older Amontillado Solera.

The process is now almost entirely one of oxidation. The butts will be kept somewhat fuller than those in the Fino Soleras, probably at about 90% capacity, but still with a very loose bung closure at the top.

Now, unlike Fino in Soleras there will be some evaporation, and from now on a light, but quite natural increase in alcohol levels will take place. The other principal factors are a gradual increase in colour levels through oxidation of the remaining glycerine, and a concentration of the naturally occurring salts in the wine. Once again, just as in Fino Soleras, the process of saca and rocío will ensure the consistency of the style being made.

There are Bodegas, González Byass being a good example where there are many levels of Amontillado Soleras. Here, the youngest Amontillado will be part of the entry point La Concha blend, but then the Tio Pepe Fino Solera is used to refresh their Amontillado Viña AB Solera, which in turn refreshes the fabulous Amontillado Del Duque Solera, which, when bottled has an average age of over 30 years. At each of these quality levels there is usually a decreasing number of butts in each stage of each Solera.

Data Source – B. Domecq Williams
– Sherry Uncovered

Table 3

Amontillado Solera Development

	Average Age, Years	Alcohol %	Total Acidity in Tartaric	Volatile Acidity g/l
Solera Fino	4	14.9	3.8	0.10
Solera Fino Amontillado	6	16.0	4.2	0.35
3rd. Criadera Amontillado	8	16.5	4.4	0.40
2nd. Criadera Amontillado	10	17.3	4.8	0.45
1st. Criadera Amontillado	12	18.0	4.9	0.50
Solera Amontillado	14	18.3	4.9	0.52

Lustau produce Los Arcos Amontillado which has 5 Criaderas and a Solera which has 87 butts, and from which the wine is bottled, but that Solera is also used to refresh the youngest Criadera of their Amontillado VORS 30 year old, and there are then a further 5 Criaderas and finally the Solera itself from which the final wine is bottled. There are just 30 butts in this Solera. Los Arcos retails at around £17 in the UK and by comparison the VORS wine retails for around £65 per 50cl. bottle. As back up for general blending of top end Amontillados for private labels and other purposes, Lustau also hold a stock of almost 600 butts of mature Amontillado, which is constantly being blended and replenished as part of their general commercial activities.

One often sees very old and rare Sherries labelled as, for example Amontillado 1/6. This denotes the fact that there are just 6 butts in that particular Solera. Lustau, again have a fabulous Amontillado de Sanlúcar from Almacenista Manuel Cuevas Jurado, which is labelled as 1/38.

Table 3 below shows a typical evolution of an Amontillado solera:

Acetaldehyde mg/l	Glycerine g/l	pH	Dry Exract	Colour 470nm
400	0.2	3.13	12	0.125
175	0.1	3.11	12	0.150
180	0.8	3.10	14	0.150
170	1.1	3.08	16	0.200
180	1.3	3.07	18	0.230
182	1.5	3.07	20	0.280

Palo Cortado Soleras

Palo Cortado is perhaps the most difficult Sherry to describe in terms of its origins and Solera management. The official description of Palo Cortado, as defined by legislation dated November 2011 is: "Amber to mahogany in colour, with aromas similar to those of an Amontillado, but a palate more similar to an Oloroso, as a consequence of its oxidative ageing once the initial film of Flor had disappeared." There is no stipulation regarding the length of time the wine must have been kept under Flor, nor how long the oxidative ageing should have lasted.

In a cynical world it would in theory be possible to blend Oloroso with a little Fino, and perhaps a touch of Amontillado, hold the blend together in butt for a short while and bottle it as Palo Cortado. So long as the aroma and flavour parameters were compatible with the above description, the alcohol level was between 17 and 22% and the sugar level below 5g/l, it would be legal. The reality is, however very different in almost all cases.

Data Source – Bodegas Fundador

A Typical Palo Cortado VORS Analysis

Alcohol	19.3	%
Total Acidity (in tartaric)	5.96	g/l
Volatile Acidity	0.78	g/l
Dry Extract	4.4	g/l
Total SO2	6.4	g/l
pH	32	
Acetaldehyde	135	mg/l

There are established Palo Cortado Solera systems, some of them of great age, and of great complexity. Notable examples can be found in such diverse Bodegas as Tradición, Williams and Humbert, Sanchez Romate and Cayetano del Pino.

Here the youngest criaderas in the system will be fed with Finos of some complexity and whose organoleptic characteristics were losing their almondy freshness, a little oxidised, perhaps on purpose, not refreshed for example for up to 12 months, becoming ideal component wines to be entered into the Palo Cortado system. Then the unique Palo Cortado Solera system takes over, but the wines never lose their lightly autolytic aromas, whilst developing into wines which are distinctly Oloroso in character but with the Fino/Amontillado characteristics beautifully delineated.

The finest Palo Cortados are eminently distinguishable from fine Amontillados. As can be seen from the Amontillado development table above, a mature Amontillado will have an acetaldehyde level of close to 200 mg/l, whereas a Palo Cortado of the same age will show a level of 100 mg/l or even less, due almost entirely to its comparatively much shorter time in biological ageing which is where the higher levels of acetaldehyde are created. True Palo Cortados are almost always much softer and rounder than Amontillados of a similar age through a greater evolution of glycerine in oxidation.

There is a certain view that the rules need a little tightening, and indeed there are some relatively inexpensive Palo Cortados on the market, but to taste wines such as the Cayetano del Pino Palo Cortado Viejísimo 1/15 butts – indicating a finished Solera of just 15 butts, or the Bodegas Tradición VORS 30 year old, is one of wine-tasting's sheerest delights.

Since Palo Cortados can be made in so many different ways, and have so many variations of complexity, it would be impossible to offer a theoretical development chart, but the chart opposite shows an analysis of a VORS Palo Cortado offered for sale by one of the major shippers.

Oloroso soleras

Oloroso Sherries are aged entirely in an oxidative process. From the moment they are designated as Oloroso at the time of the first classification, fortified to 17% and the Flor killed off, their entire evolution is influenced by air, oak, and the Solera system in which they are aged. Once in the system, as can be seen from Table 4 below, all the analytical parameter measurements from alcohol to colour intensity increase, with the sole exception of acetaldehyde, through water evaporation, but also because of the unique fractional blending process of the Solera systems themselves.

Just as with Finos, Amontillados and Palo Cortados, as young wine is blended with slightly older in these systems it gains in complexity and takes on the profile identity of the wine into which it has been fed. Olorosos develop more rapidly than biologically aged wines and can be put to commercial use sooner. Blends of inexpensive Cream and Medium Dry Sherries will contain Oloroso elements which have been aged for the minimum permitted time, and which are relatively simple on the palate, but which still represent particularly good value for money.

Data Source – B Domecq Williams – Sherry Uncovered

Young Oloroso Solera Development

Further along the evolutionary process though, these wines become more and more complex, elegant and refined as their component parts concentrate even further and they develop an exceptional tanginess, assertiveness and grip. However, as the chart shows, the glycerine content is

	Average Age, Years	Alcohol %	Total Acidity in Tartaric
Young wine just fortified	0.0	18.0	5.15
Oloroso at 3 years old	3.0	18.4	5.27
2nd. Criadera Oloroso	5.0	18.6	5.38
1st. Criadera Oloroso	6.5	18.8	5.47
Oloroso Solera	8.0	18.9	5.59

also increasing, and there develops a beautiful softness of character. This, in a well aged Oloroso, even before VOS or VORS status is achieved, creates a wine of exemplary elegance, with complex nutty aromas and flavours followed by a wonderful soft finish.

Most Olorosos are aged in Jerez, where the ambient temperatures are hotter for more of the year than in El Puerto or Sanlúcar, and the wines develop their complexity more quickly.

Among the classic examples are: Lustau's Emperatriz Eugenia Solera Gran Reserva and Valdespino's Don Gonzalo Oloroso VOS 20 year old.

However, Osborne's Sibarita VORS 30 year old and Gutiérrez Colosia's Oloroso del Puerto, along with Oloroso Faraón from Hidalgo – La Gitana, which can be found in either a standard or a VORS 30 year old version, are all very high quality examples of Oloroso from the two coastal towns. They are lighter in body and structure, but still have a nutty elegance which typifies Oloroso Sherries.

Volatile Acidity g/l	Acetaldehyde mg/l	Glycerine g/l	Dry Exract	Colour 470nm
0.31	101	6.8	20.1	0.117
0.36	94	7.2	22.8	0.194
0.39	88	7.6	23.9	0.246
0.42	83	8.0	25.0	0.291
0.46	79	8.3	26.7	0.237

Sweetening and Other Wines

All wines made from the fully fermented Palomino grape are totally dry, and their colour is entirely natural from their development in the Solera production process. Several component wines may be used to sweeten or increase the colour of any of the dry styles of Sherry, and many of them have their own separate Solera systems, whilst others are aged or simply stored in static systems.

The more common of the two naturally sweet wines is Pedro Ximénez, or P.X. and the less common one is Moscatel. In both cases the grapes are laid out to dry and shrivel on esparto grass mats out in the vineyards. As they dry out, water is lost and the sugars concentrate. When they are effectively raisins, the grapes are pressed and fermentation is started. Given the high sugar levels the yeasts are only able to convert a small percentage into alcohol, somewhere between 4 and 6%, before fermentation stops naturally. Fortification is then done to around 15% or 16%, and the wines enter their own Solera systems. As they age they concentrate in both colour and sweetness, and they are used from any age level within their Soleras to be blended with Palomino wines to create "Medium" sherries with sugar levels anywhere between 5 and 115 g/l, and "Cream" sherries with sugar levels ranging from 115 to 140 g/l. Table 5 shows a typical evolution of a Pedro Ximénez Solera.

Data Source – B Domecq Williams – Sherry Uncovered

The blending processes for the creation of Medium and Cream Sherries will be dealt with in more detail in Chapter 7.

Most Bodegas now market a single varietal P.X. which must have a minimum sugar level of 212 g/l., but which in reality

Table 5

Pedro Ximénez Solera Development

	Average Age, Years	Alcohol %	Total Acidity in Tartaric
Vintage P.X	1.0	16.00	3.30
3rd. Criadera P.X.	2.0	16.10	3.50
2nd. Criadera P.X.	4.0	16.05	3.45
1st. Criadera P.X.	6.0	16.00	3.60
Solera P.X.	8.0	16.10	3.75

often reach 450 to 550 g/l. There are one or two single varietal Moscatels on the market, and these have a minimum sweetness level of 160 g/l., but more usually register somewhere in the range of 325 to 375 g/l.

The other principal sweetening agent is Rectified Concentrated Must (RCM), purchased from commercial rectifiers, and which is water white in colour and used to sweeten almost all Pale Cream Sherries – sweetened Finos, which will have a final sweetness level of between 45 and 115 g/l.

Another wine based product which can be added is known as vino de color, or colour wine. This product is used less now than in the past, but it still has a use in Sherry blending, both for its colouring effect and for its particularly distinctive aromatic characteristics. These are principally of dark toffee, treacle and molasses, but with some black pepper and allspice. It is made from a blend of 2/3 arrope, which is grape must boiled down to 20% of its original volume over a fire, and 1/3 non-fermented Palomino grape must. There is a very slow fermentation, and the wine eventually comes out at around 9%, with a sugar level of around 12g/l. It can be aged as a single vintage or through a Solera, and with time becomes intensely viscous and as black as treacle. A tiny amount in a blend has a remarkable effect of the final colour of the wine.

Almacenista Juan García Jarana has an amazing 6 butt Solera of Vino de Color Viejo, which we always taste at the very end of a tasting, and then go for a beer!

Volatile Acidity g/l	pH	Total Sugars g/l	Colour 470nm
0.40	4.60	450	0.160
0.42	4.60	455	0.264
0.45	4.64	462	0.310
0.50	4.70	477	0.360
0.55	4.70	475	0.405

7

Selection of the Blend

General Parameters

In excess of 99% of Sherry production is fractionally blended through the Solera System. The balance is Añada or Vintage Sherry, which very few producers bring to market. Examples of exceptions are the very specialised Vintage offerings of Williams & Humbert who, from 1920, initially for reasons of internal interest and research, separated a single butt of young wine from their El Álamo vineyard in Balbaína Pago, and simply left it to develop unblended. The current owners took this concept onwards a step in 1986 and started a small vintage collection, mainly of Finos.

Production is very limited and the results are rather more of intellectual than commercial interest. The most recently released is from the 2009 vintage, and is labelled as a Fino. The alcohol level is 15%, and it is said not to have been fortified, which I somehow doubt. However, when last tasted in the Spring of 2017 it showed a clean, nutty, autolysed nose, with some, but very little fresh yeastiness. The palate was full, almondy and showing just a hint of oxidation, but would have made a perfect companion to a dish of something like grilled tuna.

Lustau also have a small collection, with small quantities isolated in what they designate to be particularly fine vintages. The most recent release is of the 1997 vintage. These wines are from specific vineyard parcels and fermentation is arrested when the alcohol level reaches around 7% when they are fortified up to around 20%. They are therefore lightly sweet and cask ageing gives them a lovely hint of spice.

Commercial Parameters

In addition to fractional blending, many Sherries are either vertically or horizontally blended; or both. Taking Finos as a first example, whilst Sherries such as Tio Pepe, Lustau's Puerto Fino and Barbadillo Solear are pure examples of finished Solera Fino styles, there is a cost involved in

keeping Sherry in Solera all the way through to its finished quality and complexity levels, and the retail price of these wines reflect that cost.

In order to create a less expensive, but still high quality Fino, perhaps at a lower retail price carrying the Bodegas own name, or as a high end private label, the blend might be as follows:

Solera	Fino	15%
2nd Criadera	Fino	70%
4th. Criadera	Fino	15%

This would still have good Flor and autolysis notes, but be less complex in terms of acetaldehyde levels, and still have some glycerine content to create a slightly less assertive finish. It would also cost less. So long as the legal parameters of selling no more than 40% of that entire Solera a year were met, this is a very sound commercial option. In fact, at a retail price point equivalent to between £5 and £7 in the U.K., this is, I believe, one of the best value white wines in the world!

Similar concepts exist in respect of Amontillado and Oloroso blends.

A fine Amontillado such as Valdespino Tio Diego will be a pure expression of that Solera, but comes at a relatively expensive price, but still very good value for money.

To create a quality sub-brand or a House Brand, we might see something like:

Solera	Amontillado	60%
3rd. Criadera	Amontillado	20%
5th. Criadera	Amontillado	10%
2nd. Criadera	Fino	9%
5th. Criadera	P.X.	1%

The resultant blend would have <5g/l sugar from the very young P.X. so still be entitled to the Amontillado designation.

For a lesser value wine with similarities of style, the blend components would be younger; there would be a higher percentage of Fino and a higher level of sweetness, therefore negating the Amontillado designation, but becoming a Medium or Medium Dry Sherry.

Cream Sherries at entry point levels will have a mixture of component parts, the majority of which will be young Oloroso, but with contributions from Amontillado, Fino, P.X and perhaps some Vino de Color, at varying levels of maturity; whereas top of the range Cream Sherries will almost invariably be blends of just Oloroso and P.X., with some considerable complexity and depth. Fine examples include such wines as González Byass Solera 1847, Lustau Capataz Andrés Deluxe Cream and Hidalgo-La Gitana Oloroso Abocado Alameda.

The options are almost unending, so long as the 40% rule is adhered to and the correct descriptors used on the label.

Sweet Blend Soleras

It is often assumed that all sweetening of Sherry, by whichever agent, is done right at the end of the ageing process, just prior to bottling, perhaps with a short time in wood once the blend is done, to marry the components together. While this may be the case in the main for entry point and lower priced Sherries, it is most certainly not always so.

The world's leading brand of Sherry, Harvey's Bristol Cream is a blend of Fino, Amontillado, Oloroso and P.X. and the components are brought together when still quite young, and travel as a blend though their own, albeit short Solera system, to ensure perfect homogeneity and consistency of style over the years.

Another world renowned brand, Williams and Humbert's Dry Sack is also blended at a very early stage, in this case Amontillado Oloroso and P.X. are aged in separate Soleras for three years, blended and the definitive blend then aged for a further three years it its own Solera system before bottling.

However, there are also some magnificent long aged sweet wines which are created in the same manner. Perhaps one of the best known is González Byass Apóstoles VORS. This is a Palo Cortado, blended at 12 years old with a similarly aged P.X. in a proportion of 87% to 13%. This blend is then aged for a further 18 years in its own Solera, to create the most opulent, elegant sweet Sherry imaginable. It is in beautiful balance with 20% alcohol, 50 g/l residual sugar and a surprisingly high acidity of 6.2 g/l in tartaric. Yes this is a Palo Cortado, but in my opinion would perhaps be better classified in the now seldom heard category of "Amoroso" – lovingly sweet!

González Byass also make a VORS Cream Sherry, marketed under the Matúsalem brand. This is a 75% Oloroso and 25% P.X blend, brought together at 15 years average age and aged for a further 15 before release. A truly exemplary Cream Sherry.

There are many other examples to be found, and I would single out Lustau Old East India for special mention, but perhaps the most unexpected delight is Osborne Solera India. In this instance the Oloroso is sweetened with very young P.X. at about 75/25 proportions, when both are at just around one year old, and the sweetness level then is just 15 g/l. Through long, long ageing in Solera and purely through evaporation of the water in the wine, that level rises to 45 g/l. The result is delicate, delicious and delightfully surprising.

8

Age Dated
Sherries

VOS and VORS Sherries

Because of the complexity of the fractional blending done in the Solera system, the very concept of an age dated Sherry was until recently seen with a deal of difficulty. However, modern technology, principally using carbon dating techniques has now allowed a much more precise declaration of average age to be contemplated.

After many years of experimentation and testing, in 2000 the Consejo Regulador introduced two new categories which shippers could use on labels, but only once exhaustive and rigorous analytical tasting and organoleptic assessment had been carried out. Both categories were given acronyms which conveniently match in both Latin and English.

The younger of the two is VOS, standing for Vinum Optimum Signatum, or Very Old Sherry, denoting wines with an average age of 20 years or more; and VORS representing Vinum Optimum Rare Signatum, or Very Old Rare Sherry, which may only be applied to wines with an average age of 30 years or more.

Qualifications for these designations are rigorously controlled.

Firstly, to qualify for VOS status, the bodega must prove that for each litre of wine of this style it wishes to sell in any particular "saca" year, it has at least 20 times as much stock of that particular wine in its corresponding Solera system. For VORS Sherries the figure is 30 times as much.

In addition the bodega must submit samples for each and every saca it wishes to make, and those samples are tasted by a committee of tasters drawn from members of the Consejo Regulador itself, as well as acknowledged industry experts. Furthermore the wines are submitted to independent analysis for elements such as carbon-14, levels of ester, ash and dry extract.

Only Amontillado, Palo Cortado, Oloroso and Pedro Ximénez Sherries are eligible for either of these designations.

There is an important dispensation in the Consejo Regulador's rules regarding the purity of these wines. Given that dry wines of this minimum age can tend to be a little astringent, they may be "enhanced" with very small quantities of sweet wines, usually Pedro Ximénez, to take the edge off that astringency, but never in such a quantity as to significantly diminish or conceal the character of the original dry wine, be it oloroso, amontillado or palo cortado in the judgement of the Tasting Committee.

These wines represent a tiny, but significant percentage of the wide range of Sherry wines. Nevertheless by virtue of their exclusive, minority nature they serve as standard bearers for the quintessential craftsmanship, selectivity and respect for time that Sherry wines encapsulate.

Not all Sherry producers submit wines for these certifications on the grounds that some of their venerable old Sherries have a much higher average age than this, and they believe that to certify them as just 30 years old would do them a disservice. In this case, no average is offered in labelling, purely a product name and perhaps the words "Very Old Sherry"

12 and 15 year old Sherries

In 2003 The Consejo Regulador introduced a further, parallel classification for slightly younger wines, called Vinos de Jerez con Indicación de Edad, meaning Sherries with an Indication of Age. Two tiers were introduced – 12 and 15 year old.

Unlike VOS and VORS the age indication applies to the Solera of each wine taken as a whole, rather than the wine of one single saca, as is the case in VOS and VORS wines. In this case the tasting and analysis is done on an annual basis and sales are limited to one twelfth or one fifteenth of the total stock held of each wine. Again, only Amontillado, Palo Cortado, Oloroso and Pedro Ximénez styles are eligible.

9

Finishing &
Bottling

Preparation for Sale

Notwithstanding many shippers' desire for minimal intervention prior to bottling, in most cases it is absolutely essential to ensure that wines stay bright in bottle and do not start to throw a sediment.

In the case of Finos, as most of them are now bottled at 15%, it is vital that everything possible is done to prevent any possibility of re-growth of Flor, once the bottle is opened and oxygen regains contact with the wine. Once the final blend has been made and any further harmonisation of the blend in casks has been completed, the wine must be made ready for bottling. This process has two main phases, the first being tartrate stabilisation, and the second filtration.

All wine contain quantities of a chemical called potassium bitartrate, which is a chemical compound found naturally in grapes, and which is in solution in the final wine. Its problem is that if the wine is subjected to temperatures of below around 4°C – 6°C, perhaps during transportation or in a domestic refrigerator, that liquid crystallises and a deposit of fine glass-like particles can be seen in the wine. Those crystals remain in solid form even when the wine is brought back to room temperature, and are often seen by consumers as a fault, and a cause for complaint.

The technology of preventing that perceived fault from occurring has changed over time, and modern methods are less aggressive than those first implemented 50 years ago or more. Then, wines would have been chilled down to between -6°C and -8°C, the higher the alcohol value, the lower the temperature, and held at that temperature for around 7 days. They have all involved chilling the wine, but the most modern methods chill the wine less, and for a shorter time than previously. The most modern technology involves packing crystals of potassium bitartrate into the conical base of a vertical tank, and wine, cooled to around 0°C is pumped upwards through the crystal bed. The stabilised wine can then be drawn off the top. The process is quicker and less aggressive than in the past, and goes some way to assuaging the doubts of the minimal interventionists.

The second process, that of filtration is less contentious, but as Sherry has spent so much of its life in butt, in contact with wood and a relatively large amount of lees in the bottom of the butt, there are bound to be some solid particles floating in the finished wine. Some producers wish to remove these particles, so as not to court customer complaints, others do not. The most prevalent way this is done is through membrane filters, of a lower or higher porosity depending on each producer's perspective on the problem.

Sadly there is a growing number of Sherries, mainly Finos and Manzanillas which are being carbon filtered. This process is used to remove unwanted colour from wines, and often renders these Sherry styles almost water white, which it seems is regarded as something of a fashion statement. Unfortunately however, in the process of removing colour pigments, some complex aromas and flavours are also lost, producing a rather bland finished wine, which, to my view is not what Sherry is all about!

Most Sherries are now bottled in an inert atmosphere, with no oxygen present, usually using nitrogen gas. As mentioned previously this is particularly important when bottling Finos and Manzanillas, but it is also of key importance when bottling even sweeter Sherries at higher alcohol levels. Sherries with an alcohol level of 17.5% and with sugar levels of say 20-35 g/l are unstable from a microbiological perspective, and great care is needed during the bottling process. Sherries may be bottled using either a driven cork, a cork stopper or a screw-cap closure.

10

The Consejo
Regulador

A Very Modern Consejo Regulador

Avenida Alcalde Álvaro Domecq, 2
11402 Jerez de la Frontera
+34 956 332050
www.sherry.wine

The Consejo Regulador "Jerez-Xérès-Sherry" was originally formed in Jerez in May 1933, and was given full legal status by the Spanish Government on 19th. January 1935. It was the first officially created to regulate what was the first ever Denomination of Origin for wines in Spain, and its founding principles have been the model for all those which have followed.

Enshrined in law are its five guiding functions:

- *The industry's inter-professional organisation*
- *Establishes the rules of the D.O.*
- *Guarantees the authenticity of the wines produced*
- *Acts as "custodian" of the D.O.s collective assets*
- *Organises Industry-wide promotion, product quality dissemination, training, marketing and communication.*

Its Mission Statement is "To be an institution at the service of the "Marco de Jerez", which is modern and transparent, capable of offering quality services, at a suitable cost, using agile management systems and qualified personnel, and at the same time to act as Ambassador for our Denominations of Origin and safeguarding their assets, identifying opportunities and contributing to an increase in its prestige, image and worth".

Its full title is – Consejo Regulador de las Denominaciones de Origen Jerez-Xérès-Sherry, Manzanilla – Sanlúcar de Barrameda y Vinagre de Jerez. To fulfil the first 4 of its 5 functions, it maintains all the registers of vineyards, vines planted, the soils they are planted on, as well as those of

Bodega stocks, movements and rotations. In addition its sets maximum yields in vineyards, production per kilo of grapes, and minimum levels of alcohol in base wines. In the bodegas it oversees stock rotations, to stipulate maximum depletions in any one year, as well as monitoring the veracity of any age dated claims. It also issues the seals of origin which must be applied to all bottles of Sherry put on the market.

It is however in its final function where over the last decade or so it has excelled. In 2015 it had a total budget for all expenditure of just over 2.5 million Euros. Of that total in excess of 1.5 million Euros were spent on promotional activities of many types. Almost 250.000 Euros were spent on activities such as Trade Fairs and general PR, and 1.4 million Euros on specific Sherry promotional activities worldwide. Similar sums were spent in 2016 and are expected to be authorised in years to come, to continue to develop the work done so far this century to reinforce the pleasures of these wonderful wines.

Its greatest achievement in 2015, during the celebration of its 80th. Anniversary of its constitution was the creation of an on-line training and education forum which during the year put in excess of 8.000 students through specific training courses.

Its new website www.sherry.wine was the first website in the world to embrace the .wine file ending.

Its **International Sherry Week** activity which was embraced by many importing countries world-wide won the "Best Digital Campaign" in the marketing of wine awarded by the UK published "Drinks International" magazine.

In May 2015 The Centre for Enhanced Development of Oeno-Tourism was opened to the public, and it sets out a very visual and audiovisual view of the Marco de Jerez as a wine tourism destination.

On an ongoing annual basis it also arranges and hosts the "Copa Jerez" competition for Sherry and Food pairing. Over a three day period Chefs and Sommeliers from selected hotels or restaurants from around the world gather in Jerez to cook a menu, designed by them and match it to Sherries they feel best marry with their chosen dishes. The Sherry and menu selection is then judged by a panel of industry experts and the winning team chosen. Truly a spectacular way to showcase Sherry and Food pairing at the very highest culinary levels. In 2017, celebrating the 7th. year of running the competition, the winners were from the Dutch restaurant Podium Onder de Dom in Utrecht, whilst the best dessert pairing award was won by The Ritz in London.

11

Principal Producers & Shippers

Producers

In this section it is not my intention to list every single producer or shipper.

The selection which follows covers, in my opinion, the most important producers and shippers, who are the most visible and operational in world export markets. It also includes the most important Almacenistas, viewed from the same perspective. The list has been compiled in no particular order.

The Sherries described in each case are a snapshot of the particular Bodega's offering and are a mixture of the most commercially relevant along with personal favourites. Mention will also be made of the more important producers of Sherry Vinegar, as this is becoming an increasingly visible part of their portfolios, and many mainstream retailers are now actively promoting it as an important culinary item.

A Typical Sherry Vinegar Solera

The Bodegas of Jerez de la Frontera

"Bodegas de Crianza y Expedición"

Producer - Shipper

Bodegas de Crianza y Expedición is often translated as Ageing and Exporting Bodegas, and Exporting taken as meaning Exporting to foreign markets. In reality the word "Expedición" is more closely linked to the verb "to expedite", in other words to move into the consumer side of the supply chain, under their own name. In my view, a more accurate description is Ageing and Shipping Bodegas

Until recently bodegas with "Expedición" status were obliged to hold a total stock of at least 2,000 butts (of 500 litres). That requirement was reduced in 2013 to 500 butts, which has meant that some of the larger Almacenistas, such as Maestro Sierra and Cayetano del Pino in Jerez, and González Obregon in El Puerto are now able to sell under their own branded names, rather than having to sell their finished wine to an "Expedición" Bodega such as Lustau, and have it marketed in a way described below in the Lustau Bodega Entry.

Bodegas Rey Fernando de Castilla S.L.

Calle Jardinillo 7-11
11404 Jerez de la Frontera
+34 956 182454
www.fernandodecastilla.com

Located in a venerable old Moorish building in Calle Jardinillo, at the heart of the Gypsy Quarter – The Barrio de Santiago, this is one of Jerez's most exciting smaller sized operations. Since 2000 it has been owned by a group of investors, who acquired it from the Andrada-Vanderwilde family, and is managed by Norwegian born Jan Pettersen, one of those investors, and who previously ran the Osborne winery in El Puerto. The Bodega in essence produces two ranges of Sherries, although in fact they overlap somewhat. The younger "Classic" range comprises a very Jerez style Fino, nutty and very almondy, as well as a Manzanilla bought from a couple of Almacenistas, a very good entry point off dry Amontillado, a very pleasant Moscatel and a clean, elegant P.X.

It is however in the "Antique" range that Jan has pulled together a stunning range of Jerez gems. The Antique Fino celebrates the style of wine which Jerez regularly had on offer when I started my career. Fuller in body than most modern Finos, with tremendous notes of autolysis, delivering brioche, almond and a certain toastiness. It is fortified to 17% alcohol just prior to bottling, and bottled with minimal filtration, having been aged through 4 Criaderas, but has an average age of around 8 years. In many people's eyes, it is really a Fino-Amontillado, and when paired with a classy plate of Jamón Ibérico and a dish of dried almonds, it truly sings.

Even better, but extremely scarce is the Fino En Rama. This is bottled just once a year, usually in May or June, with a maximum of 1.400 litres taken from selected butts of the Antique Solera, and bottled into just 3.600 half bottles, but remarkably retailing for just around £10 for one of those half bottles. Delicious. Both these Finos are bottled with minimal intervention – a gentle filtration and just 24 hours cold stabilisation, as opposed to the usual, more commercial 8-10 days.

The Solera of Antique Fino also feeds the Antique Amontillado Solera, coming in at third criadera level, producing a finished wine which averages slightly more than 20 years. This too is bottled just once a year, in winter, allowing the winter temperatures to act as stabilisation agents, and with a simple plaque filtration. It is elegant, concentrated and supple.

The Antique Palo Cortado is, if anything even more special, and even older. It could in theory be labelled as VORS, but Pettersen is not a great believer in that (or the VOS designation) and prefers to let the wine do the talking. It is an exceptional example of Palo Cortado; aged biologically for almost 10 years before being introduced to the Palo Cortado system. The autolytic notes are bright and refreshing whilst the oxidative influences create a spectrum of hazelnuts and walnuts, finishing long and satisfying.

Finally the Antique PX, which was one of the original specialities of the previous owners is rich in figgy, raisin flavours, but manages not to be too overpowering, and has a wonderfully balanced unctuous finish.

The winery is small in scale, but big in stature and class. It is also one of the very few Sherry houses which produces a range of Brandies distilled from Palomino wines, as opposed to bought in distillates from other parts of Spain. These too ooze class.

There is also a remarkable selection of 5 different Sherry vinegars, from a 5 year old Vinagre de Jerez Tradicional to a quite remarkable La Bodega Reserva Vinagre de Jerez 16 year old, to which is added 10% P.X.

Emilio Hidalgo

Calle Clavel 29
11402 Jerez de la Frontera
+34 956 341078
www.emiliohidalgo.es

A family owned concern, founded in 1874, and located from the outset in Calle Clavel in the old centre of Jerez. Now in 5th. Generation ownership. Emilio Hidalgo buy in their base wine from long term, trusted and high quality outside sources, principally from the quality Pagos of Añina and Carrascal, and runs many of its soleras from those originally laid down at the beginning of the business.

The entry point Fino is good, solid Jerez Fino, but its elder cousin Panesa Fino is quite exceptional. It has an average age of around 15 years at bottling, and would in its early years of commercialisation have been termed a Fino-Amontillado. That said it has much more brioche and almondy autolytic character than anything else, so the Fino descriptor fits well. It is minimally filtered and not cold stabilised.

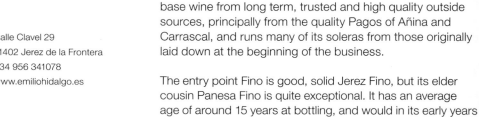

From one of the company's original Soleras comes El Tresillo Amontillado-Fino, which is perhaps one of the finest of its kind available, and gives rise to the majestic El Tresillo Amontillado Viejo 1874, which has massive concentration of hazelnut, cedar and coffee from its oxidative ageing, but still retains a fabulous freshness from the biological phase. The Oloroso Seco Villapanes is beautifully complex, offering power, structure, length and finesse. There is also an exceptionally good vinegar Solera.

Álvaro Domecq

Calle Madre de Dios
11401 Jerez de la Frontera
+34 956 339634
www.alvarodomecq.com

Although the Domecq name is almost as venerable as that of Sherry itself, Álvaro Domecq, in his second incarnation as a Bodega owner, is relatively new on the scene. When he was just 20, he was appointed Managing Director of the family company, but when that was sold to the UK firm Allied-Lyons, he returned to his first love – horses. He purchased the old premises of Almacenista Pilar Aranda in 1999, when she retired from the business, and set about turning a very soundly structured, but small Bodega into a rather more boutique affair. It is, in fact owned by a raft of cousins and small shareholders, some of whom also own small vineyard plots which supply some of the base wines. Other wines are judiciously sourced from a selection of Almacenistas.

The winery is immaculate in both its attractive presentation and the quality of its wines. General Manager José Manuel Anelo and winemaker Ana Real have put together a fine selection of wines. There is a relatively simple but very sound range of entry point wines, with the star wines Fino La Janda, out of 6 criaderas and a Solera, with good Flor and buttery autolytic notes and good long almondy finish, and Oloroso Alburejo at 18.5%, with an average of 15 years. This has an excellent concentration of natural grape salts, is bone dry, but with soft glycerine tones over the walnut dryness. A long, long finish with a fine Oloroso bite.

The Álvaro Domecq Reserva 1730 VORS range is fine indeed. The Amontillado and Oloroso are excellent, but my stand out wine is the Palo Cortado. At 21% it is high in alcohol, but the balance is in fact perfect. Soft, hazel nut, coffee cream, mocha nose. Long and deep. Massively concentrated on the palate, which is tending towards Oloroso, whereas the nose is more Amontillado. Really a fine Palo Cortado with exceptional complexity. Hazels, walnuts, torrefacto, with a great natural savoury concentration. A long sipping wine.

There is a PX Reserva 1730, but which is neither a VOS or VORS for commercial reasons. Figs, orange peel, candied fruits and raisins on the nose. Soft and long on the palate. Very complex dried fruit flavours of fig, sultana, prune and raisins over a backdrop of orange and candied peel. A long, deep finish, with exemplary acidity.

The Napoleon Vinagre Viejísimo, from a Solera laid down in 1846 is an absolute joy.

Williams and Humbert

Carretera Nacional IV, Km 641
11408 Jerez de la Frontera
+34 956 353406
www.bodegas-williams-humbert.com

Founded in 1877 by Alexander Williams and his brother in law Arthur Humbert. It was run by those two families, with offices and Bodega in Jerez, and a international sales office in London, in the wonderfully named thoroughfare of Crutched Friars close to the Tower of London. In 1972 the business was purchased by Rumasa. The business and all its stocks of Sherries were moved from the old town centre Bodega in 1994 to the premises of Bodegas Internacionales, on the outskirts of town. At that time both W&H and Internacionales were parts of the now defunct Rumasa Group of companies.

Once Rumasa had folded, there was a brief flirtation with Bodegas Barbadillo, which did not quite work out, and in 1998 the business was purchased by The Medina Group, and is still run by them, with Rafael Media as CEO, Cristina Medina as Communications Director and Paola Medina as Technical Director.

W&H own some 240ha of vineyards, 140ha in Añina Pago and a further 100ha in Carrascal. These provide for around 35% of their commercial needs, the balance being purchased either as grapes or as young wines from co-operatives and independent producers. The grapes from their own vineyards are, in the main used to create the base wines for their own brands, and those bought from outside sources, as well as the young wines purchased after harvest are used to produce the base wines for their very important private label business.

All the grapes are pressed at a dedicated press area called Las Conchas, some 6km outside Jerez in the middle of the Añina Pago vineyards. The juice is then brought down to the Jerez Bodega complex for fermentation. This is done using only wild yeasts and no further additives.

The ageing Bodega is an amazing construction, possibly the largest single winery building in Europe, with a storage capacity of close to 70.000 butts, all on one level, and ingeniously designed so that any rain is caught and held on the roof, and then distributed down inside the hundreds of conical columns which support the structure, thereby maintaining constantly balanced levels of humidity and temperature.

Commercially speaking, the most important brands in the Williams & Humbert portfolio are Dry Sack Medium and Canasta Cream. Dry Sack is a blend of Amontillado, Oloroso and PX, which are aged in separate Soleras for three years, then blended together and aged for a further three years in the Solera Dry Sack. This is a cracking Medium blend with good notes of hazelnut, toffee, toasty cedar and raisins.

Canasta Cream is a blend of Oloroso and PX, again aged separately to begin with, but once blended again aged in its own Solera for a further five to six years. A bright cream Sherry showing touches of mocha, molasses and spice. Both these wines are widely distributed worldwide.

Recently released is the delicious Canasta VOS, at 20 years average age, in 50cl bottles. It is a very separate offering to Canasta Cream and will be launched in markets where the latter is not distributed. This is Jerez Oloroso at its walnut nuttiest, with the tiniest touch of aged P.X. to soften that palate drying walnut skin astringency.

The first wine ever shipped by W&H, in 1878, was Fino Pando. This continued to be one of the company's mainstay brands until 2002, when it was re-branded as Dry Sack Fino. This has been recognised as a commercial error, and the Pando name was reinstated in 2017. The name was created to thank the shipping company which brought those first butts to London for bottling – P and O Ferries. It is a bright, relatively light Fino, notwithstanding its 5 year average

age, with a very distinctive autolytic Flor character. W&H Fino Collection, at around 8 years old is altogether a firmer, more rounded wine, with a long, deep finish. Although not owning Bodega property in Sanlúcar, W&H are able to offer two Manzanillas, selected from different Almacenistas. The younger, and to my mind the better is Manzanilla Alegría, zesty, crisp and tangy, at around 4 to 5 years old, where the W&H Collection Manzanilla is more in the Pasada style, still lively but with a certain nuttiness on the finish.

In dry, oxidative styles there are two wines which stand head and shoulders above the rest – Jalifa Amontillado VORS which is rich, complex and fragrant, with still a fine bright autolytic note from its biological phase; and my favourite Dos Cortados 20 year old VOS Palo Cortado which is bold, full bodied and particularly elegant.

Altogether different, but extremely elegant is a Medium Sweet Amontillado named "As You Like It", a fine old Amontillado, very lightly sweetened with high quality PX. And just a tickle of fine Moscatel. Bottled in limited edition 37.5cl. bottles.

Finally, the range boasts two straight PX wines. W&H Collection 12 year old which is rich, raisiny and smooth, and the altogether more complex Don Guido VOS 20 year old Pedro Ximénez, unctuous, with overtones of dried figs, dates and creamy toffee. A particularly warming wine.

Grupo Estévez

Carretera Nacional IV, Km 640
11408 Jerez de la Frontera
+34 956 321004
www.grupoestevez.es

This amazingly complex Group started its wine business life in 1974 when its founder, José Estévez, a native of Jerez, who had made a great deal of money in the business of silica mining, purchased the Almacenista business of Félix Ruiz, based close to the centre of Jerez. In 1982 he then acquired the bodega and the soleras of Marques del Real Tesoro, again in the centre of Jerez, and after a further 7 years, with the business growing exponentially created a new vinification, storage, bottling and warehousing plant on the outskirts of Jerez, which is where the existing business is run from.

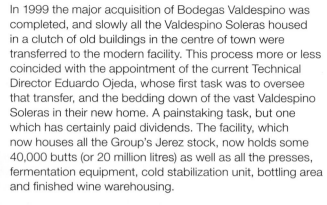

In 1999 the major acquisition of Bodegas Valdespino was completed, and slowly all the Valdespino Soleras housed in a clutch of old buildings in the centre of town were transferred to the modern facility. This process more or less coincided with the appointment of the current Technical Director Eduardo Ojeda, whose first task was to oversee that transfer, and the bedding down of the vast Valdespino Soleras in their new home. A painstaking task, but one which has certainly paid dividends. The facility, which now houses all the Group's Jerez stock, now holds some 40,000 butts (or 20 million litres) as well as all the presses, fermentation equipment, cold stabilization unit, bottling area and finished wine warehousing.

In 2007 the Sanlúcar Bodegas of Rainera Pérez Marín (La Guita) and Manuel Gil Luque were purchased. Naturally those bodegas, and their respective Soleras and other facilities are still in Sanlúcar.

The company owns almost 800ha of vineyards – 260ha in Macharnudo, 57 in Añina, 22 in Carrascal, 380 in Lomopardo and 60 in La Mariscala. From these vineyards they are self sufficient in grapes for all their Jerez production. To supply the grapes for the wines of Sanlúcar there are long term contracts with two co-operative suppliers – Miraflores and Covisan. The Manzanillas are made exclusively from Sanlúcar sourced grapes. Sr. Ojeda is a great believer in the importance of terroir in his wines. Production of Valdespino branded wines and those in the Real Tesoro portfolio is kept strictly separate.

The principal Valdespino brand is Fino Inocente, which is made exclusively from grapes grown in the Macharnudo Alto vineyard, which has some of the finest Albariza soil in Jerez Superior. The brand was first launched and registered in 1894. It was then, and still is, barrel fermented. It has a Solera system of 11 stages, unusually long for a Jerez Fino, and runs in parallel with the Amontillado Tío Diego Solera, into which it feeds after stage 8. The Tío Diego Solera also has 11 stages, 10 Criaderas and the Solera itself. Each of these 22 stages contains 70 butts of Sherry. From a stylistic point of view this delivers two remarkable wines; a particularly complex, long, yeasty autolytic Fino and a remarkably delicate hazelnut, biscuity Amontillado.

The principal Real Tesoro brand is Fino Tio Mateo, run from a solera of just three criaderas, producing a lighter weight, zippy, zesty Fino. It is from the Real Tesoro stock holding that Grupo Estévez supplies almost all its private label sherries, which account for somewhere in the region of 50% of the Group's sales volume.

Their interests in Sanlúcar are well covered. Not only with their purchases in 2007 of the Rainera Pérez Marin and Manuel Gil Luque operations, but also with the purchase of Valdespino came access to the wines of Almacenista Manuel de Argüeso, which Valdespino had acquired as far back as 1972. There are currently 3 Manzanillas available, La Guita, from Rainera Pérez Marín, a classic savoury Guadalquivir wine, as well as the rather more mineral Deliciosa, and a relatively recently launched Deliciosa en rama, which is a delight. Both these wines are aged in the delightful old Sanlúcar Bodega in the Calle Misericordia.

The purchase of Valdespino not only brought Inocente and Tío Diego into the Estévez portfolio, but also a clutch of exquisite old oxidatively aged wines, albeit in rather limited quantities. The Palo Cortado Viejo C.P. is refined, deep and darkly seductive and the Cardenal Palo Cortado VORS is simply sublime. Then there is the truly astonishing Niños Pedro Ximénez VORS, which compares to any other I have ever tasted. That these wines were transferred in tact from the old Valdespino Bodegas in Calle Ponce is due to a great extent to the loving care given to them in both their original home and the new Bodega by bodega foreman José Luis Monje.

There are also 3 Sherry vinegars available, all of them very well made, but by far the best of them is Valdespino Vinagre de Jerez Superior.

González Byass

Calle Manuel María González 12
11403 Jerez de la Frontera
+34 956 357000
www.gonzalezbyass.com

By a distance the biggest producer of biologically aged Sherries. These include Tio Pepe and all its Fino, Amontillado and Palo Cortado criaderas and Soleras. There is a separate short Solera system for the entry point Fino marketed as Elegante, and another completely separate, also short Solera system for Croft Original and Croft Particular. The raw materials for these three maturation systems are separated at harvest time, with different quality musts being selected for each, prior to fermentation. In all the Bodega has just over 30,000 butts in stock, of which 20,000 are in biological ageing.

The flagship brand Tío Pepe is the world's biggest selling Fino, and its production base has created such gems as the wonderful Fino Dos Palmas. Tío Pepe is a classic, well structured Jerez Fino, with a fine autolytic backbone, rich minerality and a lingering finish. It is created from 22 separate Solera systems in different locations throughout the Bodega complex; which are blended together in varying proportions to create the final blend. Walking through the Bodega, the marginally distinct temperature and humidity differences in all the buildings become noticeable, and the reasons for the complex structure of the wine become vividly evident. González Byass pioneered the new wave of "en rama" – straight from the cask finos, with minimal intervention, when it launched Tio Pepe En Rama in 1994. This is winemaker and Master Blender Antonio Flores pride and joy. A selection is made each year from the final Solera level butts in each of the 22 separate Tío Pepe Solera systems. Once the designated butts have been selected, a total of just under 9.000 litres is withdrawn, in equal proportions from each butt, to be bottled without stabilisation or filtration.

The Author (left) with González Byass Master Bender – Antonio Flores

The Amontillados are equally good. Viña AB which is fed indirectly from the Tio Pepe Soleras via 600 butts of Fino Amontillado and in which the Flor is allowed to die naturally, creating a relatively low alcohol Amontillado at 16.5%. Viña AB itself has a final Solera of 120 butts, part of which is bottled, but some goes to refresh the youngest criaderas of the classic VORS Amontillado Del Duque, but which is also refreshed from a series of Amontillado-Fino nurseries which have been developed expressly for that purpose, but which are never bottled commercially. The Solera of Amontillado

del Duque also has 120 butts. It is a massively complex system of ageing which seems to defy commercial logic, but which is part of the rich heritage of this remarkable company.

In addition, again delivered from specifically designated biologically aged sources there come the recently launched Palo Cortado Leonor, and the stunning Apóstoles VORS Palo Cortado. Leonor was first released in 2010, and is around 15 years old, relatively high in alcohol at 20%, but beautifully balanced in autolytic, hazelnut and walnut flavours, but with a light touch of ginger on the finish. Apóstoles is an all together different proposition. It is initially fed from the Leonor Solera into the youngest part of its own Solera, which was laid down in 1862, in honour of a visit from the then Queen of Spain, Isabella II. The butts for this Solera are old PX butts, and Apóstoles matures here for a further average 15 years, culminating in a richly complex wine, unique to the region.

There are two very elegant Olorosos in the range, Alfonso, which is dry and the oxidative equivalent of Viña AB, and Oloroso Dulce Solera 1847 Cream, which is blended with around 25% P.X. at around 3rd. Criadera stage. Both Apóstoles and Solera 1847 Cream are dealt with in fuller detail in the final section of Chapter 7.

González Byass has perhaps the largest holding of Pedro Ximénez vineyards planted in the Marco de Jerez, at 27ha, and in the very best albariza soils in Macharnudo.

It is not surprising therefore that their commercial offering is outstanding. There are three groups of Soleras in the Bodega. The first creates the Nectar brand, aged for around 10 years, and which is fine rich fruity example, the second is purely a feeder Solera which is never put in bottle, but is the main nursery source for the majestic Noë, an intense, rich, deep and particularly delicious VORS P.X.

González Byass now owns Croft, the main product being Croft Original, a Pale Cream Sherry, which has its own separate, quite simple Fino Solera. Just prior to bottling the wine is sweetened with the appropriate amount of RCM up to 116 g/l, fortified to 17.5% and returned to butt for a short while, filled brim full to prevent any to unwanted physical reaction with the sweetening agent, and to harmonise the blend before bottling.

Lustau

Calle Arcos, 53
11402 Jerez de la Frontera
+34 956 341597
www.lustau.es

Founded in 1896, Lustau markets one of the most complex and complete ranges of Sherries in the region, and while being very active in the volume sales sector of house brands, is probably best known for its promotion of the concept of Almacenista Sherries. Before the lowering of the minimum stockholding requirements for Sherry houses to what they are today, it was until recently a requirement for anybody wishing to market wines under their own name to have a physical stock of more than 2,000 butts, a quantity much in excess of that commonly held by most of the Almacenistas. In the 1980s, the then, visionary, Managing Director of Lustau, Rafael Balao embarked upon the marketing concept of purchasing mature wines from a number of Almacenistas, and offering them for sale under the Lustau brand, but also indicating on the label not just which Almacenista they had been purchased from, but also the size of Solera they had been taken from.

For example one saw a Lustau branded Oloroso Pata de Gallina, from the Jerez Almacenista Juan García Jarana

1/38, indicating a Solera of just 38 butts. Lustau still list an impressive range of Almacenista Sherries, 7 in all at the time of writing, covering all three sherry towns, and ranging from Fino del Puerto from González Obregón, through the delicious Amontillado de Sanlúcar from Manuel Cuevas Jurado to the sublime Oloroso Pata de Gallina from Juan García Jarana.

The company was purchased in 1990 by the Caballero group of companies, giving it a major capital boost, and the freedom to move from its rather cramped premises in La Plaza del Cubo, built into the old Moorish walls in Jerez to the current premises in Calle Arcos, previously owned by Harvey's, who had themselves purchased the bodegas of Mackenzie and Manuel Misa. Lustau own two vineyard complexes, the most important being Montegilillo on the outskirts of Jerez, consisting of around 130 hectares of Palomino, which is complemented by the Las Cruces vineyard near Chipiona, growing mainly Moscatel.

The main Lustau brands belong to their Solera Reserva range, including, unusually a lovely trio of distinctive Finos, one from each of the Sherry towns – Manzanilla Papirusa, Puerto Fino and the Jerez Fino Jarana. These are complemented by Los Arcos Dry Amontillado, Escuadrilla Rare Amontillado, Peninsula Palo Cortado, Don Nuño Dry Oloroso, Capataz Andrés Deluxe Cream, all of which are excellent in their respective styles, and the range is topped by two excellent single varietal sweet wines, Don Emilio P.X. and Emilín Moscatel.

Most recently Lustau purchased the Domecq brands of La Ina Fino, Botaina Amontillado and Rio Viejo Oloroso, along with their corresponding Solera systems, all of which were successfully transferred to the Calle Arcos premises, under the watchful scrutiny of Capataz Manuel Lozano, who sadly passed away during 2016.

Additionally, Lustau have access to the Soleras of The Caballero Group in El Puerto, from where they source entry point offerings under the Burdon, Caballero and La Cuesta brands, as well as wines to supply to major retail groups worldwide under private label.

Lustau were one of the first bodegas in modern times to move back to producing single vintage Añada Sherries, the first being in 1990, and the latest from the 2007 Vintage.

Lustau also produce excellent Sherry vinegar.

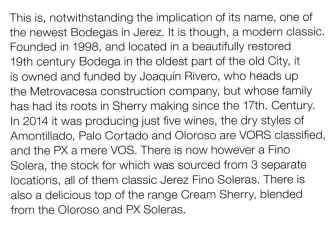

Bodegas Tradición

Calle Cordobeses, 3
11408 Jerez de la Frontera
+34 956 168628
www.bodegastradicion.es

This is, notwithstanding the implication of its name, one of the newest Bodegas in Jerez. It is though, a modern classic. Founded in 1998, and located in a beautifully restored 19th century Bodega in the oldest part of the old City, it is owned and funded by Joaquín Rivero, who heads up the Metrovacesa construction company, but whose family has had its roots in Sherry making since the 17th. Century. In 2014 it was producing just five wines, the dry styles of Amontillado, Palo Cortado and Oloroso are VORS classified, and the PX a mere VOS. There is now however a Fino Solera, the stock for which was sourced from 3 separate locations, all of them classic Jerez Fino Soleras. There is also a delicious top of the range Cream Sherry, blended from the Oloroso and PX Soleras.

The company owns no vineyards, but has amassed its stock of around 1.300 butts by assiduous purchasing, initially of the original wines to create the Soleras, and since then following a very careful replacement policy for wines to replace any which are required for bottling. As the amount of wine bottled each year was initially a maximum of 15.000 bottles, this was not a gargantuan task, but in order to replicate the quality of the Solera wines, wine must be sourced with the utmost care. Total sales in 2016 had risen to around 20.000 bottles, of which 6.000 are Fino

The size and quality credentials of the operation can be encapsulated in the fact that the Amontillado Solera system, of seven separate steps comprises just 158 butts in total, with the Solera itself having just 19 butts. Qualifying for VORS status means that the average age is over 30 years, and therefore the "young" wine entering the youngest Criadera has already to be of an advanced age, and of supreme quality. Wines are bought in either from Almacenistas, or from known Bodega sources which, for whatever reason have a surplus of stock over commercial requirements.

Everything is done by hand, including bottling and labelling, with every bottle individually labelled and numbered, the Capataz, Pepe Blandino personally supervising every step of the process. The wines are totally natural, with no additions of colour or caramel, and are not tartrate stabilised or filtered prior to bottling.

In addition to magnificent Sherries, the Bodega buildings also house part of the vast collection of Spanish paintings owned by Sr. Rivero. On my last visit I saw paintings by Velázquez, El Greco and Goya and a fascinating collection of tiles painted by Pablo Picasso when he was just 8 years of age. The Bodega collection rotates around Sr. Rivero's main collection on a regular basis. Very much worth a visit.

Bodegas Fundador

Calle San Idelfonso, 3
11403 Jerez de la Frontera
+34 956 151500
www.bodegasfundador.com

There has been considerable commercial turmoil behind the ancient walls of this venerable and particularly beautiful Bodega over the last two decades or more.

The original buildings date from 1730, when construction was started by one Patrick Murphy, who was shortly joined in his business venture by Juan Haurie y Nebout, a Spaniard with French connections and one of the renowned personalities in the history of Sherry and its commercialisation. 1816 is a key date as it was the year when Pedro Domecq Lembeye joined the business, and his descendants were to manage and develop the business for almost two centuries under the famous name of Pedro Domecq. It was a family business until 1994 when it was purchased by the British firm Allied-Lyons and was renamed Allied Domecq. Allied-Lyons already owned Harveys of Bristol

Harveys of Bristol was founded in 1796, and was one of the oldest wine merchants, not only of that English City, but also

in the UK. They created Bristol Cream in the 19th. Century, having previously marketed a successful Sherry blend named Bristol Milk. Bristol Cream became very popular in late Victorian times and was said to be a favourite of Queen Victoria herself. In those times Harveys owned no Bodegas or stocks of wine in the Jerez region, but bought from trusted suppliers who blended their Sherries for them, and shipped them to be bottled in Bristol. By 1970, Harveys was part of the West of England Cider Group Showerings, who decided that they ought indeed to have a physical presence in Jerez, and were able to purchase the long established business of Mackenzie & Co, and then in 1979 the next door Bodega complex of Misa & Co. Showerings in their turn were bought by Allied Breweries in the UK.

Domecq became defunct in the late 20th. Century and the whole business was bought by Beam USA, and later by Suntory. In 2016 the company was sold again, and was acquired by Philippine businessman Andrew Tan.

Most of the old Domecq Sherry brands, along with their corresponding Soleras were sold, either during the Allied Domecq ownership period, or during the Beam and Suntory tenures. The brands now managed by the Bodega are Harveys and Terry, the latter being principally a Brandy and Spirits operation, as well as the massively important Domecq Fundador Brandy. Bristol Cream is its flagship brand, but there is also a limited range of good quality everyday Sherries. The Fino is exemplary, at 15% alcohol,

and only bottled in 50cl. Its average age is around 5 years, very yeasty, with almonds dominating the back palate. There is also an exceptionally good top end offering of high quality VORS Sherries comprising an Old Amontillado, a Palo Cortado, a Rich Old Oloroso and a PX, which overall sells over 1,000 butts per year equivalent. In my view, the Old Amontillado is the star here. Technical Director Manuel José Valcárcel recently picked up the IWC award for Champion of Champions for this very wine.

Since Andrew Tan's arrival there has been a noticeable uplift in the spirits of the workforce, especially in the winemaking and technical parts of the operation, and it would not be surprising to see some even better wines reach the market soon. On a recent visit, I was able to taste two completely different Palo Cortados, both produced from Primera Yema, but aged in different buildings in the Bodega complex. Those from the Sacristía Bodega were lighter and finer, destined for the Harveys VORS range, and those from the El Molino building were fuller, and perhaps longer and more incisive on the palate.

Interestingly during all the commercial upheaval, the Bodega was able to retain possession of all the vineyards which originally supplied the base wines for the top end Domecq Sherries, so the supply base for the future seems secure.

Cayetano del Pino

Plaza de Silos, 3
11403 Jerez de la Frontera
+34 956 345736
www.bodegascayetanodelpino.com

Cayetano del Pino have their origins in Jerez in the late 19th. century, the family having previously run a wine wholesaling business in Sevilla, but a business failure surrounding a rogue partner at the beginning of the 20th. Century nearly broke the company. For many years they operated as an Almacenista, with poor sales and little confidence. Perhaps rescued by the Lustau Almacenista concept, the 4th. generation of the family moved the business to its current address in Jerez's Plaza de Silos just over 30 years ago. The building and some of the wines there had previously been owned by Domecq.

They produce neither Fino nor Oloroso, but are specialists in Amontillado and Palo Cortado, and have around 1,000 butts

split almost equally between each style. Amongst these butts there is a grouping of just 10 butts of Palo Cortado, set aside twenty years ago, purely for consumption by the family. These butts have not been refreshed commercially for more than 15 years, except to top up volume lost by evaporation. Very recently they decided to put some of the wine on the market. There is one "saca" per year, which is limited to 2,000 bottles of 50cl each. This is labelled simply as Palo Cortado de Jerez 1/10, and is quite delicious – rich, bright and long on the nose, with hints of almonds, hazelnuts and a touch of toffee. On the palate it is still remarkably fresh, still showing its biological origins, but layered on top there are flavours of black toffee, vanilla and exotic spices, such as allspice, cinnamon and clove, and the palate length is exceptional. Even more special is the Palo Cortado de Jerez 1/5 which was selected from the company's old Bodega Santa Ana on Calle Arcos, and which is over 35 years old. The base wine was barrel fermented, and the resultant wine is quite remarkable, perhaps one of the most complex Palo Cortados I have ever had the privilege to taste.

This Bodega often opens its doors at the weekend to showcase the local Bulería Flamenco style of singing and dancing, and which is unique to Jerez. Well worth a detour!

El Maestro Sierra

Plaza de Silos, 5
11403 Jerez de la Frontera
+34 956 342433
www.maestrosierra.com

Located just next door to Cayetano del Pino, this is yet another jewel in Jerez's crown. It was founded in 1830 by José Antonio Sierra who was also a Master Barrel Maker (Maestro Sierra!) Two generations later it was being run by the son of his wife's niece, Antonio Borrego, and when he died in 1976, the mantle of responsibility passed to his widow Pilar Plá Pechovierto, who is still alive and very much part of the enterprise, although the business management is run by her daughter Carmen Borrego.

This is a beautifully appointed Bodega, with a total stock holding of around 1.300 butts and producing a full range of Sherry styles from Fino through to P.X. Being located up on the high scarp facing down to El Puerto on the west

side of town, it is perfectly positioned for thick Flor growth to be encouraged.

They own no vineyards, but source their base wine every year from the same three sources to ensure continuity. They buy from a co-operative in the Pago of Miraflores near to Sanlúcar, as well as from another in Balbaína, and a third source well in land close to the town of Trebujena, in quite a hot climate, but tempered by the proximity of the River Guadalquivir. Each source supplies them with wines produced from the same vineyards every year, and the wines themselves are always of primera yema quality.

Of the 5 wines in their "Basic" range, as they term it, but which is far from basic, the Fino and Amontillado stand out. The Fino at 15% has a good pastry nose, good Flor influence both living flor and through the effects of autolysis. Clean and bright, mid lemon yellow, quite full yet soft on the nose. A very, very good, ripe bready Fino. The Amontillado at 17% is light and soft on the nose, with some nougat, and very pronounced aromas of hazelnut. Clean and very incisive on the palate, again, bags of hazelnuts, and a very long, warm, appealing finish.

It is, however, in their range of Vinos Viejos, that Maestro Sierra excel. The Amontillado 1830 VORS, at 19% is unusual, in that it is aged in some of the original barrels created by the founder, but which have a capacity of around 2.000 litres as opposed to the usual 550. This produces a wine which is more oxidative than wood influenced in style, delivering exquisite elegance and finesse. The Palo Cortado at 20% is indeed a rarity. The Solera is tiny, and in 2015 for example only 300 bottles were released. It is deep amber – mahogany in colour, with a nose initially of molasses, but with good yeasty influences behind. Deep, long and fine on the palate, with an incisive zesty finish. A truly majestic wine.

The Oloroso 1/14 at 22% is another rarity, with only 116 bottles released in 2015. Antique shop mahogany nose, followed by some deep molasses. The palate is amazingly complex, with flavours from molasses through candied orange peel to dried walnuts. A long sipping wine. Even more complex is the Oloroso Extra Viejo VORS 22%, at around 80 years old – 36 bottles. Show stopping! Deep, very deep mahogany colour. Full, rich walnut and molasses nose. The palate is initially very soft, from the concentrated glycerine, but with a very concentrated tangy bite to the tongue. The finish is long, almost non-stop, particularly warming and with a deep treacle molasses aftertaste.

Sanchez Romate

Calle Lealas, 26-30
11404 Jerez de la Frontera
+34 956 182212
www.romate.com

Located at the very heart of the old part of Jerez, from a Sherry perspective, Sánchez Romate has had its ups and downs over the years, and is probably better known for its Brandies, most notably the well known Cardenal Mendoza brand. However, at the time of writing its Sherries are once more in the ascendancy. One of the oldest Bodegas in Jerez, it was founded in the late 18th. century by Juan Sánchez de la Torre, and was run by his descendants and their relatives until 1954, when it was sold to a group of local friends and investors, who took the company on a decidedly brandy focused course. Descendents of those families still own and run the Bodega, and in the last 20 or so years have regenerated the Sherry side of the business. They were perhaps encouraged by the fact that documentation was discovered which showed that in the early 20th Century Sánchez Romate held the Warrant for supply of Sherries to the British House of Lords.

A stroke of good fortune came their way at the tail end of last century when, having expanded sales and stocks, they were considering moving to newer premises on the outskirts of town. The Bodegas next door, which had previously been owned by the now defunct Sherry shipper Wisdom and Warter came up for sale, and they were able to purchase not only the buildings, but some interesting stocks of Sherry.

The core range of wines is known as The Reservas Especiales Range. The excellent start point is Fino Marismeño, a classic Jerez Fino averaging about 7 years in age and bottled, with just a light filtration at 16%. Rich and rounded yet still quite steely, it has lovely autolytic notes from the relatively long ageing under flor, yet still has plenty of elegant apple notes and a lovely toasty almond finish. The Marismeño Solera feeds the quite delicious Amontillado NPU – an absolute textbook classic Jerez Amontillado.

Averaging around 13 years of age, it has hazelnuts, toffee, mocha and a touch of fig on the nose, but with still a bright autolytic undertone. The palate is bone dry, long, steely and beautifully structured. The Oloroso in this range called Don José is a classic Jerez walnut and torrefacto wine. However the two stand out wines here are the honey and orange blossom sweet Moscatel Ambrosia and the Pedro Ximénez Cisneros which is long, deep and very refined.

Sánchez Romate has recently launched a newly developed pairing of Fino and Amontillado. The Fino is called Fino Perdido 1/15 butts (lost Fino) from a very infrequently refreshed Solera Fina known as Celestino, and the Amontillado Olvidado 1/5 toneles (forgotten Amontillado), from just 5 larger than usual barrels of some 600 litre capacity, giving a slightly fuller level of oxidation, and which had been left untouched for over 20 years. The latter is in very limited availability, and most of it is allocated to The Wine Society in the UK. It is bottled at 20% alcohol and sells for £16 per 37.5 cl bottle. Truly majestic!

Urium

Calle Muro, 28
11404 Jerez de la Frontera
+34 956 335597
www.urium.es

The Ruiz family, father Alfonso and his live-wire oenologist daughter Rocío are relatively new to Jerez, but have announced themselves in quite spectacular fashion. Originally from the town of Moguer in Huelva province, on the Atlantic coast close to the border with Portugal. Alfonso had a life-long dream to own and run a Sherry Bodega, and in 2007 purchased an old, existing Almacenista bodega in the very old part of Jerez, close to the cathedral, on the Calle Muro, along with some 500 butts of rare old Solera Sherries.

In the intervening period they have expanded those stocks with some judicious acquisition of young and old wines to complement the original wines and to create a particularly balanced proposition of mid to high end wines, named as Clásicos along with a superlative set of VORS wines. All base wines are bought in from one single source, the Finca Blanquita vineyard property in Añina Pago. The Clásico range includes a memorable fuller weight Fino, which whilst only being bottled en rama at 15%, delivers amazing Jerez Fino complexity of almonds, brioche and yeasty autolytic notes. The location of the Bodega, almost on the top of the ridge which faces down towards El Puerto is perfect for extended Flor development during most of the year, and which is vital in creating this complexity. The Amontillado and Palo Cortado in this range benefit too from this location, both being on the more biological than oxidative side of life. The Amontillado especially, at an average 15 years old is superlative. The is completed by also an Oloroso and a P.X, which are particularly sound wines.

It is in their VORS range however that the Ruiz family have shown their true passion. Again the Palo Cortado and the Amontillado are stand-out wines in their categories. The Palo Cortado is exemplary. At around 40 years average age, it is a wine with great grip, classic in its remaining hints of autolysis whilst showing notes of hazelnut, rich toffee, allspice and cinnamon over a fine, long dry walnut finish.

This is Jerez at its very best.

Almacenistas

The word Almacenista has its etymological origins in the Moorish language. "Al" is the definite article in Moorish, the Moorish word "makhzan" means storehouse, giving us macén and the final syllable in Spanish means "a person who does something" – so we have a storehouse keeper. These would have proliferated in Jerez in the 15th, 16th. and 17th. Centuries before the evolution of bigger commercial players, and many of the businesses which are now shipping Bodegas, such as, for instance Maestro Sierra, González Obregón and even Lustau started life as Almacenistas. They are still a vital link for many Bodegas looking to source small quantities of wine either to make up a blend or to replenish a Solera system with a particular style or quality of wine.

The principal Almacenistas of Jerez are as follows:

Juan García Jarana

This tiny Bodega, located in a corner of Plaza del Cubo in the old Santiago district of Jerez is a gem. Juan García's "day job" is as a distributor of top of the range motorbikes throughout Andalucía, although Sherry is his passion. He holds stock of some amazing Solera wines, from Fino all the way through to P.X. and all of them are delights.

His Fino, of which the biggest customer is Viniberia, is a Jerez classic. At 18%, with a rich almond nose, good ripe Flor notes and a discernible autolytic tanginess is perfect with a plate of Jamón Ibérico; and the palate goes on for ever. This wine refreshes the elegant Amontillado Solera, and the result, not unexpectedly is a fine hazelnut offering, with a steely grip and lovely length.

Perhaps the star of the show in his Oloroso Seco "Pata de Gallina" which has been marketed for years by Lustau, since the inception of its Almacenista range in the early 1980s. Pata de Gallina means hen's foot in Spanish, and is given to a perfectly Dry Oloroso where the high glycerine levels are more prevalent than the concentration of natural salts brought on by concentration though evaporation in Solera. It retails at over £20 per 50cl bottle, but is well worth that and more.

Vides S.A.

Vides, with cellars and offices in Calle Ancha, also in the Santiago district, is something of a Palo Cortado specialist. The business was founded in 1958 by Tomás Domecq Rivero, a scion of two noble Jerezano families with generations of Sherry tradition. It is now managed by his grandson Fernando León Manjón Domecq.

The grapes for all their wines are sourced from one specific vineyard the "Esparta" in the Carrascal Pago.

They are best known for their Palo Cortado de Jerez 1/50, which is distributed in 50cl bottles in the Lustau Almacenista range. It has a rich toffee, marzipan and dried fruit nose, with some sweet chestnuts behind, and some leathery touches. The palate is zesty and zippy, with some wonderful allspice and cinnamon notes and more leather. Polished and refined this finishes with some bright black pepper and a warm glycerine aftertaste. It retails for a little over £20 for a 50cl bottle.

Visits to both of these Almacenistas are trade only or strictly by appointment through their respective distributors.

The Bodegas of El Puerto De Santa María
Bodegas de Crianza y Expedición

González Obregón

Calle Zarza, 51
11500 Cádiz
+34 956 856329

Bodegas González Obregón is something of an institution in El Puerto. It is in its 4th generation of family ownership, and was originally an Almacenista, but has been registered and a fully fledged Bodega de Crianza y Expedición since 2005. It was first brought to prominence as one of the Lustau Almacenistas in the 1990s, with an absolutely exquisite Amontillado del Puerto, but there truly is much, much more to it than that. Located in the Calle Zarza at the top of the town, the warmest part of the town, it does have a lovely Fino, but its Amontillado del Puerto and its Palo Cortado are exemplary. The Soleras are tiny but the generosity of the two brothers who run it is amazing. The doors are always open, to trade and consumers alike.

Total stock holding is a mere 600 butts, of which in excess of 500 are Fino and Amontillado del Puerto. They buy in Sobretablas wine every year from the same independent grower and winemaker who has vineyards and a press house just over a kilometre away to the north of the town.

There are always wines to taste in the tiny premises; and to buy in bulk (take your own bottle or flagon if you wish)! And on Saturdays they open for lunch, cooking simple local country foods in season – wonderful rustic stews in winter, and fresh fish from the Bay of Cadiz all year round, paired with the finest of El Puerto Sherries. Free range chicken in a P.X. sauce washed down with a half bottle of Amontillado del Puerto – Delicious!

Bodegas Gutiérrez Colosia

Avenida Bajamar, 40
11500 Cádiz
+34 956 852852
www.gutierrez-colosia.com

This lovely bodega, still in its original 1838 premises, which was expanded to its current size in the late 1960s, is an absolute gem. Located just across the road from the wharves along the River Guadalete, just before it empties into the bay of Cadiz, it was also originally an Almacenista, but under the careful management of Juan Carlos Gutiérrez, great-grandson of the founder, it has been bottling wines under its own name since 1997.

The bodega produces a very complete range of Sherry styles, from young to venerable, but perhaps the most striking is the Fino Puerto, which is a classic of its style. The Finos of El Puerto logically fall somewhere between the heavier weight, more autolysed wines of Jerez, and the tangy zest of Sanlúcar. They are lightly autolysed, but still bright and refreshing; quite fruity. Fino Puerto is sold as El Cano in some markets, but the wines are exactly the same. It is just an average of 4 years old, but shows a lovely refreshing complexity. There are hints of apple and almonds in among the yeasty flor flavours, and it has wonderful length. The very distinctive flavours created by the Bodega's location are carried through into the Amontillado del Puerto and the Oloroso del Puerto, both tangy and elegant with the Oloroso especially delicate. Superlative mid priced wines.

At the top of the range is the Solera Familiar range with a strikingly good pairing of Amontillado and Oloroso, 50 and 35 years old respectively, but the star of the show is the even older Palo Cortado which is taut, fine, elegant and has unstoppable length, still with noticeable hints of flor, but the concentrated finesse of an aged Oloroso. Finally there is the most amazing PX, from a Solera laid down in the 18th. Century. Gutiérrez Colosia bottle less than 500 x 50cl bottles of each of these wines every year, but they are well worth looking out for. On principle they do not apply the VOS and VORS labelling concepts as they believe them to be too constraining, but their top of range wines still show the finesse and beauty of long aged Sherries.

Osborne S.A.

Fernan Caballero, 3
11500 Cádiz
+34 956 869000
www.osborne.es

Osborne is now part of a major multi-national foods and beverages company, and its Bodegas in El Puerto have the most up to date technology. Its history, though, is fascinatingly and inextricably linked to the great surge in international commercial interest in the region in the 18th. and early 19th. Centuries. Through marriage and family links to the now defunct Duff Gordon, Thomas Osborne Mann, and later his son Thomas Osborne Böhl de Faber effectively had control of the business by 1836, and were sole owners by 1872, selling wines under both the Osborne and Duff Gordon brand names, the former mainly in Spain, the latter in export markets. The wines are still very good, although somewhat overshadowed by Brandies and other wines.

The famous Osborne Bull can be seen in hundreds of different sites throughout the Spanish countryside. It used to be the symbol used to advertise their Veterano brandy, but was prohibited in that use in the late 1980s, and there were plans to pull all the scaffolding structures down. This met with outcry, and they became protected sites – albeit without any mention of the product they used to advertise.

The standard range is known in house as the Premium Range, and head winemaker Marcos Aguacil is understandably particularly proud of it. It is all made from primera yema wines from grapes grown in Balbaína, and a total of 300,000 litres is made annually. The best known and most widely available is Fino Quinta, which is delicious. A classic, everyday drinking Puerto Fino, soft bright and tangy, with plenty of Flor influence and a pleasant savouriness. Next in complexity is the very fine Coquinero, which Sr. Aguacil refers to as Fino Quinta's big brother. It is in fact a Fino-Amontillado, and has been labelled as such for so many years that the Consejo Regulador has given Osborne permission to continue using this descriptor, even though it is not allowed for in the 2011 legislation. Only 6,000 litres are bottled each year. The brioche and autolytic notes from the Flor are predominant, but there is just a touch of elegant nutty oxidation around the back of the nose and palate.

The Bailén Dry Oloroso at an average 8 years old also sings out El Puerto from the very beginning. It is clean, bright and remarkably sophisticated at 20% alcohol. Both the nose and palate show hints of tobacco, some allspice and cinnamon and a touch of cocoa. The clever winemaking here has been to hold the wine in Sobretablas, but at 18.5%, for well over a year, and then to feed it into the Solera scales which are at 20%. Only 20,000 litres a year are released to market.

When Bodegas Pedro Domecq was subsumed into Beam Global, they sold off huge chunks of Soleras and their accompanying brand names, initially to their Pernod Ricard arm who subsequently sold them on to Osborne. Osborne then sold on the more every day brands and Soleras of Fino La Ina, Amontillado Botaina and Oloroso Río Viejo to the Caballero Group, but sensibly kept the jewels in the crown.

There are four wines in this brand range layer, and all of them have VORS status. The first is the Amontillado 51-1a VORS which is stylish, complex, detailed and long. A classic of its style, but still with a beautiful lingering El Puerto influence. Sibarita Oloroso VORS, was marketed as a Palo Cortado by Domecq, but has been converted to an Oloroso by Osborne. It is rich and opulent in all senses, enhanced by the fact that is lightly sweetened to 9 g/l with a gentle dose of old Pedro Ximénez – permitted under the VORS regulations. The true Palo Cortado VORS Capuchino is one of the lightest I have tasted, almost milky in its texture,

reminding of coffee cream, brioche but with a subtle walnut backdrop. It is on the edge of Palo Cortado, almost veering back towards Amontillado. This collection is closed off by a cracking, concentrated, raisin, chocolate and dried fig Pedro Ximénez appropriately named VORS Venerable.

However, as sweet Sherries go, from a personal point of view, the very best Osborne offering is Solera India. This is an Oloroso sweetened with P.X very early in life, and which spends its ageing span in a sweet Oloroso Solera. In this Solera, as the ageing process carries on, the level of sweetness rises from just 15 g/l up to 45 g/l purely through natural evaporation. There is a fine, rich delicacy of sweetness here.

Juan C. Grant S.L.

Bolos 1 y 3
11500 Cádiz
+34 956 870406
www.bodegasgrant.com

Founded in 1841 and previously classified as an Almacenista, with the recent stock-holding conditions relaxed, Grant is now a fully fledged ageing and shipping Bodega. Located around 5 blocks up town from the Guadalete River, not surprisingly their forte lies in finos and other Sherries with developed biological ageing. Fino Garrocha, light and youthful, is a classic Puerto Fino, full of Flor nuances built around a lovely citrus, almost lime blossom fragrance. Its Amontillado sibling, also branded Garrocha, and at almost three times the average age still has lovely Flor undertones, but a complex hazel nut and marzipan note.

Grant source their base wines for these and the delicious Amontillado and Oloroso Viejos from producers whose grapes are grown along the coast, mainly around Sanlúcar, as well as in Chipiona, so it comes as no surprise that they have a superlative, delicate still lightly terpenic Moscatel. It is beautifully aged but still retains the finesse of its youth. Grant's wines are not widely distributed, but very much worth looking out for.

Luis Caballero S.A.

San Francisco, 32
11500 Cádiz
+34 956 851751
www.caballero.es

Luis Caballero is no longer registered as a Bodega de Crianza y Expedición, but the buildings in the old Bodega in Calle San Francisco are still full of Sherry. These are mainly the feeder Soleras for the many private label customers the group supply, as well as some of the Soleras which feed Lustau brands, such as Lustau Puerto Fino. They also own brands such as José de la Cuesta and Burdon, which are used as secondary brands for multiple retailer sales. The quality is exemplary, and from a purely commercial point of view, I believe they sell some of the best quality everyday entry point Sherries to be found, especially in Finos and young Amontillados. Caballero also own the old Moorish Castle in El Puerto, Castillo de San Marcos, which is well worth a visit.

There are currently No Almacenistas registered in El Puerto

The Bodegas of Sanlúcar de Barrameda

Remarkably there are almost as many registered Bodegas de Crianza y Expedición in Sanlúcar as there are in Jerez and El Puerto together. However of the 19 registered in Sanlúcar in 2016, very few are well known in world markets. This is probably accounted for by the difference in sales trends in the domestic and export markets for Manzanilla as compared to Finos de Jerez and Finos del Puerto.

In 2016 Total global shipments of Finos were registered at just over 7.6 million litres, of which 31% was consumed in Spain. By comparison shipments of Manzanilla in the same year amounted to just over 7.1 million litres, of which 92% were consumed domestically, with just 8% shipped to the rest of the world. Consumption of Manzanilla in Sanlúcar is much higher than Fino in either Jerez or El Puerto, and the market for Manzanilla in the city of Sevilla is massive.

There are historical reasons for this, in that the River Guadalquivir is perfectly navigable up to Sevilla, and in the 19th. Century barges would convey Manzanilla in bulk, along with the fish and shellfish of the town up to Sevilla to market. By comparison, it was always easier to get Jerez wines down to either El Puerto or Cádiz for export shipment than it was to transport wines internally by road north. The road from Jerez to Sevilla was rife with banditry.

Bodegas de Crianza y Expedición

Bodegas Barbadillo S.A.

Luis Eguilaz, 11
11540 Sanlúcar de Barrameda
+34 956 385500
www.barbadillo.net

Bodegas Barbadillo is a family owned and run winery, established in 1821 by Begnigno Barbadillo Hortigüela who was originally from Burgos in Northern Spain. It is now run by the 7th generation of his descendants, and is without doubt the largest producer of Manzanillas. They own some 400ha of vineyard in the inland district of Gibalbín, on very high quality albariza soil, and, most importantly cooled by the Poniente wind which blows directly off the sea to the southwest. It is perhaps confusing that these vineyards are at least 30km from Sanlúcar, but as head winemaker Montse Molina explained, the important issues are healthy, phenolically ripe grapes, not too high in potential alcohol, harvested quite early in the season, with relatively low levels of total acidity, and low levels of gluconic acid, and crushed as soon as possible after picking. In addition to the owned vineyards, Barbadillo also manage a further 600ha throughout the Jerez Superior region.

The vinification plant is also at Gibalbín, and is used to crush and ferment all the grapes from the total 1,000ha. After reception at the winery the grapes are crushed if necessary – for the hand harvested grapes only, and passed though "Desvinadores" – sieve-like semi-cylinders. This process delivers some 60% of the total juice, without pressure. This free run juice is allowed to settle naturally for 24 hours and then centrifuged to remove solids and sent to ferment in stainless steel tanks for between 10 and 12 days at 17°C. until all the fermentable sugar has been converted into alcohol. The young wine is fortified to 15% to allow the Flor to grow, and is held in bulk storage at the Gibalbín facility, until it is needed to refresh the youngest of the scales of the Soleras in Sanlúcar.

The principle product of Barbadillo is Solear Manzanilla. There are some 11,500 butts in total through 10 separate stages. Interestingly at Barbadillo these are known as "Clases" or Classes rather than Criaderas and Soleras, although the classic system of fractional blending is the same. Each Clase however is held in separate buildings in

the very distinctive winery complex. The winery is at the top of the town, in the Barrio Alto, overlooking the river below. Each of the buildings has a marginally different internal climate in terms of temperature, humidity and aspect to the river. Over many generations it has been discovered that each of these buildings offers differing attributes to the maturing Sherry, the coolest and most humid being the most appropriate to house young wines where the Flor is most active. As all the butts of one Clase are kept together in the same building, not only does this assure total homogeneity within that Clase, but also makes the business of running the scales much more exact and labour efficient. The 10 levels of ageing means that Solear is one of the oldest and most complex Manzanillas sold in the market, with an average age of between 6 and 7 years

The final Clase (or The Solera) is used not only to bottle Solear, but also to feed the tiny production Solera of Manzanilla Pasada, which produces just 4,000 half bottles a year, from 4 separate "sacas" one in each season. Logically the Manzanilla Pasada Solera is also used to feed the Amontillado Principe Solera, at around 15 years old, and this, in its turn feeds the magnificent Amontillado VORS Solera which has an average age of around 40 years; and beyond that the incredible Reliquia which is bottled in minuscule amounts.

There is a limited edition of Palo Cortados and Olorosos, and an absolutely stunning Pedro Ximénez, the Solera of which is also used to create their delicious Cream Sherry, blended in tiny quantities with some lovely old Oloroso.

Hidalgo – La Gitana

Banda de la Playa, 42
11540 Sanlúcar de Barrameda
+34 956 385304
www.lagitana.es

It would be difficult to be closer to the River Guadalquivir and its beach than this magnificent Bodega, built in the early 19th. Century. It is run now by Javier Hidalgo, a sixth generation descendant of the founder José Antonio Hidalgo, a native of Cantabria in northern Spain, who had come to Sanlúcar in the late 18th Century. The company, in partnership with several members of the Hidalgo family, manages just over 200 hectares of vineyards in the Miraflores and Balbaína pagos, all on prime Albariza soils, and all within 10km of Sanlúcar itself. In the middle of those vineyards is the El Cuadrado vineyard where Hidalgo have built a pressing and fermentation plant. All the company's grapes are vinified here making it one of the few self-sufficient houses in the region. In excess of 90% of the production is destined to become Manzanilla, and the bulk of that their world famous brand La Gitana.

The company changed its name to Hidalgo – La Gitana in the late 20th Century to reflect that commercial importance, but also to clear any confusion with the Jerez based Emilio Hidalgo.

La Gitana has a particularly complex Solera system, with 14 Criaderas and the Solera itself, but each of those 14 Criaderas has several levels of sub-Criaderas, and there is a massive level of cross blending between all of those elements, purely to ensure that there is an absolutely constant supply of nutrients for the Flor to remain active all year round. La Gitana translates as The Gypsy Woman, and has its origins in a Malaga bar run by a locally famed Gypsy dancer, in which the wine had gained a certain popularity, becoming known as the special wine sold in La Gitana's Bar. There is an original portrait of La Gitana herself hanging in Javier Hidalgo's office.

La Gitana is a light, bright, savoury and crisp Manzanilla and is quite delicious with the particularly fresh shellfish and white fish delicacies on offer in the many bars adjacent to the Bodega. In fact the town's magnificent fish market is just over the road.

Hidalgo release a small quantity of La Gitana En Rama twice a year, in spring and autumn, and have recently increased its production from the original 300 bottles in 2011 to almost double that in 2015.In 1997 Hidalgo released the first bottling of their newly crafted Manzanilla Pasada – La Pastrana. It is a single vineyard offering from their eponymous vineyard in Miraflores, and is a rich, nutty, complex wine with just a touch of autolysis and oxidation to balance the classic Manzanilla tang.

The older, oxidised styles of Hidalgo Sherries are a delight. Most of those Solera wines are housed in a small section of the Bodega, which is below street level, in fact below river level, and with its own very special mini climate. The Duke of Wellington Palo Cortado, locally known as Jerez Cortado is especially good, as is the Napoleon Amontillado VORS, also created from wine of the La Pastrana vineyard.

Delgado Zuleta

Avenida de Rocío Jurado S/N
11540 Sanlúcar de Barrameda
+34 956 360133
www.delgadozuleta.com

Said to be the oldest wine company in the Marco de Jerez, first registered in 1744 by its founder Francisco de Ledesma. The current name of Delgado Zuleta relates to one María José Delgado Zuleta who married a descendant of the founder, and took over the reins of the business at the end of the 18th Century.

In 1985 the company started the process of merging the 12 separate Bodega buildings it owned in various parts of the town, by building 3 completely new modern bodegas, linked to each other, but on three different levels in a part of Sanlúcar known for its high levels of humidity, facing west into the Poniente wind, on rising ground, with a clay subsoil and with a high water table, close to the river. It was something of a Herculean task, and lasted in all 16 years.

It was done in 3 separate stages, each one ensuring that the process of crianza for their Manzanillas was not compromised in any way. Being such a long established company, some of the butts which needed to be moved were particularly venerable, and the company contracted 3 coopers for the whole of the 16 year period to ensure that any butt damaged in any way could be repaired promptly, and on the spot. A total of 5,000 butts were moved to the new premises.

The business owns no vineyards of its own, but just over 50% of its needs are supplied from vineyards owned privately by members of the family. Fermentation is carried out under contract by other Sanlúcar Bodegas. Total annual production and sales currently stand at just over 800.000 litres

Delgado Zuleta markets one of the best known Manzanilla brands – La Goya. This is a classic, if slightly old fashioned

Manzanilla Pasada, although not labelled as such. This brand represents some 20% of their volume, either sold in bottle, or "en rama" in 15 litre glass carafes to the bars of Sanlúcar and surrounding villages and towns, even as far away as Sevilla. The wine averages around 7 years at bottling. It is mid green yellow in colour, with a lovely Flor zest on the nose, and plenty of bright green apple notes. Rounded on the palate, savoury but with flavours of biscuits and freshly baked bread and a good, clean long Flor finish.

There is a relatively new addition to the range – Goya XL En Rama Reposada. This is a delicious wine. Golden in colour. Autolysed nose, but still clean deep and rounded with a touch of Quince Paste – "Membrillo" – on the finish. Bone dry, long and fresh, but complex. It almost has a touch of old Jura about it. Very creamy textures on the palate and a full, dry finish.

A very recent addition is a first organic Manzanilla which has been branded "Entusiástico". Just 1,200 bottles have been released. The grapes for this wine are sourced from a single grower in the Pago of Burujena, some 10km east of Sanlúcar on the road to Trebujena, and the wine is bottled at 15%. A true delight.

A standard Amontillado at 17% is produced, which is workmanlike but not anywhere near as exciting as the Quo Vadis? XL Amontillado at 20% and somewhere between 40 and 50 years old. This has its origins in Miraflores Pago and

is fermented every year in new oak. It came into the Delgado Zuleta business with their purchase in 1978 of the Rodríguez La-Cave bodega, where it had lain almost dormant for decades. Deep amber in colour and aromas. French polish, over figs and hazelnuts, very resinous. The palate is huge, and the alcohol perhaps a little overpowering at first, but when sufficiently aerated the long estery aromas of old Amontillado start to develop into roasted figs, hazelnut toffee and some resplendent creaminess on the finish.

A further contribution from the cellars of Rodriguez La-Cave is the exemplary Manzanilla Barbiana, which in tasting terms is technically a Manzanilla Pasada, although it is not labelled as such. It is deep in almondy nuttiness, with a feel of autolysis, but still some baking bread freshness. A perfect foil to some of the firm flavoured langostinos from the Bay of Cadiz. Its elder brother Goyesco Amontillado is very much in the same vein, but deeper, nuttier and more complex, whilst still retaining its bright zest.

La Guita – Hijos de Rainera Pérez Marín

La Guita having been part of Grupo Estévez in Jerez since 2007 is dealt with fully in that company's entry in the Jerez Bodegas section of the book.

Herederos de Argüeso

Herederos de Argüeso S.A.
Calle del Mar, 8
11540 Sanlúcar de Barrameda
+34 956 385116
www.argueso.es

Argüeso is an archetypal Sanlúcar Bodega, specialising in Manzanilla Fina, Manzanilla Pasada and Amontillado de Sanlúcar. Its original premises on Calle del Mar, adjacent to the River, are still in use as Bodegas and Offices, although over almost 200 years in existence it has acquired bodegas throughout the lower part of town, as well as building a modern vinification plant further out from the centre, close to the town's ring road on the way to Chipiona.

In 2016 ownership and control passed to Sr. Francisco Yuste, a local businessman who had previously developed a relationship with the Sanlúcar Bodega Pedro Romero and had started building some brand equity with their brands. The Yuste controlled business now has access to stocks close to 10.000 butts and has ownership of the famous Las Medallas and San León Manzanillas. Of the two, Las Medallas is the lighter and younger of the two, a fine average 4 year old wine, with classic Sanlúcar savouriness, pungency and finesse – classic almond and autolytic aromas and a fine zippy palate. San León, previously referred to as Reserva de la Familia, on the other hand is, in truth a Manzanilla Pasada, but is in fact labelled as Manzanilla Clásico. It is clean, precise and very pungent, almost verging on Amontillado, which with an average age of some 9 years is hardly surprising.

There are bound to be changes in the near future as Sr. Yuste consolidates his Pedro Romero brands into the existing Argüeso business, but as a native of Sanlúcar, the impression as of now is of a desire to rebuild some of the Las Medallas and San León somewhat faded prestige.

Bodegas Barón

CTRA. Sanlúcar – Chipiona, km 1
11540 Sanlúcar de Barrameda
+34 956 360796
www.bodegasbaron.es

Barón own around 140 ha of vineyard on prime albariza soils, most of it in single estates between Sanlúcar and El Puerto. One of the Estates – La Atalaya was acquired from Osborne. The main Bodega in the higher reaches of town houses some 10.000 butts, mainly of Manzanilla, but also of Amontillado, some Oloroso and Sweeter wines, notably a delicious Moscatel.

The presentations of these wines has recently been totally revamped from a very conservative label style to a some what zany but eye catching series of designs. Micaela is the dominant Manzanilla brand at around 4 years old, zippy zingy, full of citrus and yeast, with a lovely bright long finish. One step up at around 8 years old is Xixarito Manzanilla Pasada, which is bottled En Rama and this is followed by a 10 to 11 year old Manzanilla Pasada called Soluqua. This is as close as it gets to an Amontillado de Sanlúcar, but as the boundaries between the two are so blurred and the company does not wish to lose the Manzanilla descriptor, it is labelled as Pasada. They are all quite delicious and supremely elegant.

The triple branding plan runs all the way up through the range ending with a set of three P.X. wines, a youthful Micaela, a more complex Xixarito and a truly divine Soluqua.

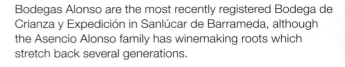

Bodegas Alonso

Bodegas Alonso are the most recently registered Bodega de Crianza y Expedición in Sanlúcar de Barrameda, although the Asencio Alonso family has winemaking roots which stretch back several generations.

Bodegas Alonso
Calle Bolsa 114
11540 Sanlúcar de Barrameda
+34 856 585530
www.bodegasalonso.com

They recently acquired the old Bodega premises of Pedro Romero, along with the most important Soleras and Criaderas of centuries old Sherry which had formed the basis of Romero's Prestige and Heritage brands as well as the Gaspar Florido brands 25 GF and Ansar Real, and the highly respected Soleras of Almacenista Fernando Méndez. The Bodega is located on Calle Bolsa, very close to the river. This is a family with a vision and a mission, offering tiny volumes of exquisite old Sherries to a very limited, but particularly fortunate client base. Their first Saca was towards the end of 2016 when they released a limited edition of 500 sets of 4 half bottles each selected from single butts of Pedro Romero and Gaspar Florido Soleras. Each set comprises two half bottles of Palo Cortado of at average ages 120 and 70 years, as well as a 100 year old Amontillado and an Oloroso of around 70 years old.

Then in 2017 they released a collection of an old Oloroso 1/14 from Pedro Romero, an Amontillado 1/15 from the Soleras of Gaspar Florido and a stunning Palo Cortado 1/8 from Fernando Méndez – all these with an average age of between 35 and 40 years, and bottled in very attractive 50cl flasks. There is also a delicious "mature" Manzanilla "Velo Flor" of around 10 years old.

I have been fortunate enough to taste all these wines and they are all truly delectable, with those of the original 2016 Saca quite spellbinding. They are also particularly expensive, but then, why sell such jewels cheaply?

Almacenistas

Following the change in regulations regarding minimum stockholdings, many of the producers previously described as Almacenistas are now categorised as Bodegas of Crianza and Expedición.

There are now just 3 Almacenistas left in Sanlúcar, most of whose names are totally unknown outside the Sherry Sector. However, one shines out as typical and has become relatively well known in the Wine Trade, due to the original marketing of Almacenista Sherries by Lustau.

Manuel Cuevas Jurado S.L.

The family's main business is that of a produce and drinks wholesaler to the local catering trade – the numerous hotels, restaurants and bars of the town and surrounding area. Their main warehouse is now on the outskirts of town, but the original premises are in a back street close to the river, where the Sherries are still kept.

The Manzanilla Fina is a gem, the Pasada even better, but the fame has come through what used to be known as the Manzanilla Amontillada, and is now Amontillado de Sanlúcar. This is a hand crafted beauty, and should be on every Sherry lover's "to have" list!

I once tried to purchase a little of his 3 butts of Manzanilla Olorosa, and was told firmly, but very politely, that it was for the family's private consumption, but then only after Mass on Sundays. Sadly old Manuel Cuevas is no longer with us, but his sons still carry on a loving tradition.

Other Important Players

There are two further businesses which must be mentioned here. They are not producers, but act in way as négociants, bringing very particular, and in many cases very exciting Sherries to market. They are Equipo Navazos, and Viniberia.

Equipo Navazos

Initially, this was not a commercial venture, rather more the identification of very special wines by its two founders, for onwards sale to the funding group of investors in the project. It was started in 2005 by Jesús Barquín, who is a criminal law professor at the University of Granada, but who is also a regular contributor to The World of Fine Wine magazine, and to the wine sections of the Spanish newspaper El Mundo, and Eduardo Ojeda, the technical director of Grupo Estévez. The two had been friends and collaborators for some years, but in 2005 located a remarkable Solera of Amontillado in the cellars of Sánchez Ayala in Sanlúcar, which had lain untouched for years. They brought together a group of likeminded investors to fund the purchase, and bottled just one selected butt from the Solera, for distribution amongst themselves.

It was such a success amongst the members that they encouraged Barquín and Ojeda to seek out similar opportunities from other Bodegas, not only from within the Marco de Jerez, but also up in Montilla. The principal suppliers have been the original Sánchez Ayala, Bodegas Pérez Barquero in Montilla, Fernando de Castilla in Jerez, and perhaps unsurprisingly, Bodegas owned and run by Grupo Estévez.

The single butt selections have been numbered chronologically from La Bota de Amontillado No 1, and as of 2016, there have been upwards of seventy single butt releases. They started to be released on to the open market as from La Bota de Palo Cortado in 2007. These are, unusual and rare Sherries, and due to their limited availability – just over 650 standard bottles of each, have become almost collectors' specialities. What is for certain is that they are all remarkable complex examples of the breadth and depth of spectrum of Sherry, and even at the rarefied prices they now fetch on world markets, they are extraordinary value for money. Berry Bros. and Rudd (BBR) of London, Hong Kong, Singapore and Japan, one of the world's foremost retailers of Fine Wine have La Bota No. 56 Pedro Ximénez on offer at £95 per bottle and La Bota No. 58 Amontillado at £55.

Viniberia

Viniberia is a very different sort of Négociant. With offices in Jerez, and a partner business in London, they are actively working with a series of Sherry Bodegas to create special, limited editions of fine and rare Sherries specifically for them. It is owned by the Dauthieu family, with Peter Jr. running the Jerez operation, and his father Peter Sr. based in London. Born and schooled in Jerez, Peter Jr. has worked in several Bodegas, has a passion for the wines of the region, and is something of a latter day Rafael Balao, constantly on the move, uncovering hidden gems, in the major Bodegas de Crianza y Expedición with which he works, for example with Sánchez Romate, with whom he has created Fino Perdido 1/15 butts and Amontillado Olvidado 1/5 toneles.

He is also at the forefront, along with Lustau, in working with the best Almacenistas to bring their wines to a wider audience. He has created a series called Pedro's Almacenista Selection wines in collaboration with Bodegas García Jarana for Fino, Amontillado and Oloroso, as well as with Cayetano del Pino for a selection of truly spectacular Palo Cortados, starting with an entry point offering at around £17 per bottle, through the truly delightful Palo Cortado Solera 1/15 butts at about £20 to a majestic Palo Cortado Viejísimo 1/5 butts at around £25 both in 37.5cl bottles.

Not only are the wines very special, but their presentation and labelling uses imagery first produced for the annual Fiesta de la Vendimia (Vintage Festival) Posters, which were designed by a different artist every year. The Vendimia Fiesta is the summit of the Marco de Jerez publicity and celebratory year, and these new labels are joyous in the extreme.

Soon to be released is a single butt Pedro Ximénez at £65 per 37.5cl. named Salto al Cielo from Bodegas Conde de Peraleja. It is named after a tiny hamlet east and slightly south of Jerez, very close to the River Guadalete and is a spectacularly beautiful place.

His truly is a labour of love, and it is to be hoped that he continues to be supported by the major retailers and specialist private supply companies with which he currently works.

12

Labelling Legislation

General Sherry Regulations

The most recent legislation on the permitted terms to describe styles of Sherry was published and came into force on 30th. November 2011. It reinforced previously enacted laws and simplified them. It was marginally updated in August 2013, and that update is reflected below. The principal purpose of the original legislation was to clarify the permitted usage of the terms Fino, Amontillado, Palo Cortado and Oloroso, as well as to redefine those styles permitted to use the word Manzanilla.

Set out below are the basic analytical parameters by style descriptor and a general note on what the different styles should look and taste like. These terms and conditions cover not only labelling, but also commercial literature used in Marketing Sales and Advertising.

Data Source - C.R.D.O. Jerez – Xérès – Sherry

Type of Wine	Alcohol by Volume	Suger Level
Fino	15% – 17%	max. 5 g/l
Amontillado	16% – 22%	max. 5 g/l
Oloroso	17% – 22%	max. 5 g/l
Palo Cortado	17% – 22%	max. 5 g/l
Dry	15% – 22%	5 – 45 g/l
Pale Cream	15.5% – 22%	45 – 115 g/l
Medium	15% – 22%	5 – 115 g/l
Cream	15.5% – 22%	115 – 140 g/l
Pedro Ximénez	15% – 22%	min. 212 g/l
Moscatel	15% – 22%	min. 160 g/l
Dulce (Sweet)	15% – 22%	min. 160 g/l

In the case of Amontillado, Oloroso and Palo Cortado styles, as a consequence of the concentration processes associated with oxidative ageing, the sugar levels may legally increase to 9 g/l, but only if the total acidity level, expressed in g/l in tartaric is not more than 2 grams per litre lower than that of those sugar levels.

The above wine styles should conform to the following attributes:

Fino.

Straw yellow to pale gold in colour, with discernible aromas and flavours of biological ageing. Its specific characteristics are the consequence of the fact that its entire ageing process has been carried out under a film of Flor.

Amontillado.

Amber in colour, of a greater or lesser intensity, with aroma and flavour characteristics developed as a consequence of its particular ageing process, of a first phase in biological ageing, followed by one of oxidative ageing.

Oloroso.

Intense amber to mahogany in colour with very distinctive aromas and flavours as a consequence of its oxidative ageing.

Palo Cortado.

Amber to mahogany in colour, with aromas similar to those of an Amontillado, but a palate more similar to an Oloroso, as a consequence of its oxidative ageing once the initial film of Flor had disappeared.

Dry.

Pale yellow to gold in colour, with specific aromas of biological ageing under Flor and a lightly sweet palate.

Pale Cream.

Straw yellow to pale gold in colour, with specific aromas of biological ageing under Flor and having a smooth palate.

Medium.	Amber to mahogany in colour with aromas bringing together those of both biological and oxidative ageing, and having a smooth palate.
Cream.	Deep amber to deep mahogany, with strong aromas of oxidative ageing, and a sweet palate.
Pedro Ximénez.	A wine made from the juice of at least 85% ripe and sun dried Pedro Ximénez grapes, with fermentation arrested by the addition of alcohol. Golden amber to mahogany in colour, of greater or lesser intensity, or even ebony. Deep and intense with aromas of dried grapes. Sweet and luscious on the palate.
Moscatel.	A wine made from the juice of at least 85% ripe and sun-dried Moscatel grapes, with fermentation arrested by the addition of alcohol. Golden amber to mahogany in colour, of greater or lesser intensity, or even ebony. Deep and intense with aromas of dried grapes. Sweet and luscious on the palate.
Sweet Sherry.	Wine made from the juice of ripe and sun-dried grapes from authorised grape varieties, with fermentation arrested by the addition of alcohol. Golden amber to mahogany in colour, of greater or lesser intensity, or even ebony. Deep and intense with aromas of dried grapes. Sweet and luscious on the palate.

Specific Regulations for Sanlúcar de Barrameda Wines

Wines with the protection of the Denomination "Manzanilla – Sanlúcar de Barrameda" traditionally known as "Manzanilla" are fortified wines whose characteristics are the result of the particular process of biological ageing exclusively in those Bodegas located in its designated "Ageing Zone". Manzanilla is pale straw yellow to pale gold in colour, with aroma and flavour specific to the process of aging under a film of Flor.

Those Manzanillas which as a consequence of extended ageing show a fuller golden colour and a pronounced structure may be permitted to use the mention – Manzanilla Pasada, but only when permitted to do so by the Consejo Regulador, following tasting verification by its Tasting Committee.

Note

The previously permitted designations of Manzanilla Amontillada, Manzanilla Olorosa and the very rare Manzanilla Palo Cortada may no longer be used. These wines must now be described as Amontillado, Palo Cortado or Oloroso de Sanlúcar de Barrameda, with absolutely no mention of the word Manzanilla on either labels or promotional materials of any sort.

13

World Markets

World Markets for Sherry

From the beginning of the 21st. Century, Sherry has addressed its position in world markets in a much more robust manner than in the last quarter of the20th. Century when high volume sales were the principal focus, often at unsustainable prices.

At the time of writing, in the previous ten years total world sales have reduced from 56 million litres to 34 million litres. In the same period however, total stocks in the Sherry Bodegas have reduced from 225 million litres to just over 130 million litres.

There has been a massive shift in emphasis from volume to quality, with biologically aged sherries part of the driving force at entry point level, and the exceptional age dated and VOS/VORS wines playing a major back-up role.

For instance, since 2006 sales of Manzanilla have risen from less than one million litres to something over 7.1 million litres, with some 20% of total sales, nearly catching up with sales of Fino which in 2016 were 7.65 million litres at 22.25% of total sales.

The commercially important Cream and Medium Sherries still sell well, but are no longer the ubiquitous face of Sherry. Sales of Cream Sherries are down from 12.5 million litres to 7.4 million litres, whilst Medium Sherry sales have dropped from 11.8 million litres to 7.16 million. These are still significantly important styles for Sherry but younger customers are being attracted to the sector by Finos, Manzanillas, Dry Amontillados and Dry Olorosos. This has been much helped by the clarification of labelling regulations which enforced maximum sweetness levels of 5 g/l on wines labelled Fino, Amontillado, Palo Cortado or Oloroso.

Interestingly sales of Pedro Ximénez did not register in the 2006 official statistics, whereas in the 2016 figures they are logged at just under 1 million litres. Sales of Amontillado and Oloroso in their newly regulated designations now account for over 3% of total sales – just over 1 million litres, which is quite a distribution achievement. Similarly, sales of Palo Cortado had not been logged as a separate style over many years, but in 2016 registered sales of almost 90,000 litres. Niche, but psychologically important from an image point of view.

Data Source - C.R.D.O. Jerez – Xérès - Sherry

Sales in 2016, by category were as follows, in decreasing order of volume (with their 2006 position to the far right):

Fino	7.65	million litres	1
Cream	7.43	million litres	2
Medium	7.16	million litres	3
Manzanilla	7.13	million litres	8
Pale Cream	2.49	million litres	4*
Pedro Ximénez	0.97	million litres	n/a
Oloroso	0.60	million litres	7
Amontillado	0.40	million litres	5

The most important markets in terms of volume are:

Spain	12.02	million litres
U.K.	9.90	million litres
Holland	5.70	million litres
Germany	2.30	million litres
U.S.	2.15	million litres
Belgium	0.70	million litres

Other European markets are important, but with lower volumes, and other world markets, notably Canada – mainly Cream Sherries; and Japan – mainly Finos and Manzanillas; also import significant volumes.

* Pale Cream is a decidedly British phenomenon, first created in the 1970s Its principal brand is Croft Original, now owned by González Byass, and most of the other wine sold is as supermarket house brand. Of the 2.49 million litres sold in 2016, 2.41 million were shipped to the U.K. – just under 97%

14

Sherry Food
Pairings

Food Pairing Suggestions

With so many styles of Sherry available and with so many levels of complexity, it is reasonable to say that Sherry is one of the most flexible wines in the world in regard to food matching.

Manzanilla Fina

Being produced at the mouth of the River Guadalquivir where it flows into the Bay of Cadiz on Spain's south west Atlantic coast Manzanilla Fina pairs absolutely perfectly with the abundance of seafood and shellfish to be found there. The fish is excellent all the way from the Straits of Gibraltar in the south up to the border with Portugal in the west. Baby prawns, razor clams, tiny cockles, sea urchins, baby soles, delicious fresh anchovies and baby squid, lightly floured and fried are all exceptional and delicious.

Manzanilla Pasada

Pairs magnificently with locally caught turbot, fresh tuna, monkfish and grouper fish, along with the local "Urta" which translates as Stone Fish, and is unique to the Bay of Cadiz. Cooked in a light tomato, garlic and red pepper sauce. Quite magnificent!

Fino

Perhaps the most versatile of all Sherries to match with foods, and because of its complex, almondy, yeasty flavours combined with the zing from the developed acetaldehyde it marries with some of the most difficult foods to pair wine with. Fresh green and canned white asparagus spring immediately to mind, as do Jerusalem and Globe Artichokes. Any Ibérico ham cut, especially ham from the leg or shoulder, with its slightly earthy flavour is ideal with chilled Fino. Olives too – local, aptly named Manzanillas, stuffed with anchovy are quite a revelation. Difficult white cheeses, Wensleydale, White Stilton and Compté are obvious candidates. Finally, but by no means least important, Fino is an absolutely natural partner to the somewhat ubiquitous, but entirely delicious Tortilla Española, a delightful combination of eggs, potato, onion and garlic, served either hot or cold, and Spain's most widely consumed Tapa.

Amontillado

Needs and combines with fuller flavoured foods. Its predominant hazelnut flavours match it perfectly with Tandoori or rich duck dishes, even a garlic roast Poussin! It is also perfect with pork or chicken liver pâté, with mushroom risotto, and almost any vinaigrette dish.

Medium

A favourite partner for Medium Sherry is Spicy Stir Fried Prawns. Quiche, especially using smoked bacon or a smoked cheese works well, as does Apple and Goat's Cheese Salad.

Palo Cortado

I first tasted a real home-made oxtail casserole in Jerez in 1970, in a restaurant just opposite the bull ring, where not unsurprisingly it was a speciality. Palo Cortado was what I was given to drink with it, and the tradition has lasted almost 50 years. They are truly sublime partners. Smoked duck and smoked venison also work, as does a classic game pie – hot or cold.

Oloroso

We have a speciality at home with wild mushrooms, or if those are not available, even shop bought oyster mushrooms will suffice. Very quickly fried in virgin Spanish olive oil, a tiny amount of garlic an a twist of sea salt, and the pan deglazed with old Oloroso. To die for! Roast pheasant works too, as does a casserole of belly pork or slow roast shoulder of hogget or mutton with shallots and lentils.

Cream

Mother used to make a magnificent lemon meringue pie, and a stunning Raspberry Pavlova. On her first visit to Jerez she rustled up a lemon meringue pie at the home of a young Bodega colleague of mine, and the combination has stuck with him and all his relations. Cream Sherry is also a great partner to Foie Gras.

Pedro Ximénez

Deliciously simple, but fine P.X. is a delight just poured over home-made vanilla ice-cream. For a more seasonal offering, served with Christmas pudding or mince pies it is a joy. Blue cheeses such as Stilton, Gorgonzola, Danish Blue, Cambazola or the Spanish mountain cheese Cabrales also match beautifully.However, to paraphrase Antonio Flores, Head Blender and Winemaker at González Byass when asked about which dessert would best pair with his amazing NOË VORS Pedro Ximénez he said "This wine does not need a dessert to pair with – This wine IS the dessert"

15

Final Thoughts

Having lived and worked in Jerez towards the end of one of the so called "Golden Ages", and having been commercially involved with Sherry in some way for most of my working life, I have seen some of the best and the worst of the fortunes of these exceptional wines.

It is now pleasant to see that there is a sense of cautious, but determined optimism and hope. The sector is now more or less back in balance in respect of production, stocks and sales. Although the last of these three areas is still in decline, there is rather more than anecdotal evidence that profits are increasing as more and more, better quality is being sold, consumed and written about. Whilst researching and writing this book, I have encountered scores of young bloggers, drinkers, sellers and winemakers who are not just ambassadors for Sherry, but who live and breathe the wines.

There have been many mistakes made along the way, and several false dawns. By way of just one example ...... In the early 1990s I was working as an EU Wine Inspector in Brussels and saw at first hand the very sad grubbing up of some of the area's best vineyards. EU rules meant that more money was to be paid for grubbing up the most productive areas of vineyard. Unfortunately those vineyards with the highest yields were those on the finest Albariza soils, producing some of the finest base wines, but as their owners had not seen much in the way of payment for years, it was too big an opportunity to resist.

Fortunately under the rules of time lapse, some of those vineyards have now been able to be replanted. Also, very fortunately, some of the vineyards which should never been planted to Sherry vines in the first place, especially those well on the way out towards Arcos de la Frontera and beyond La Barça de la Florida further south, will never again now be replanted.

We are seeing a resurgence of Sherry at high retail values, which is very exciting for all Sherry lovers. Their sales are minuscule as a percentage of total sales, but they act as standard bearers for the entire Sherry Trade, which lest we forget still sells close to 50 million bottles per year worldwide.

Sherry has its stocks to sales ratios as close to balance as is possible, at something like 3.9 years stock to sales, as of 2016, compared to an untenable position of almost 5.5 just 5 years previously. Given that most Sherry is sold at the minimum legal age of 2.5 years, that still leaves plenty of scope for the higher value, lower volume Sherries such as VOS, VORS and some of the magical Almacenista and Single Release Sherries which are catching the eye and the wallet of fine wine lovers around the world.

Most of the world's great winemaking areas are judged by their top end offerings – Vintage Port, Premier and Grand Crus in Burgundy, First and Second Growths in Bordeaux, Gran Reserva Riojas, yet all of these areas balance their books by selling huge quantities of everyday wines.

It is to be hoped that the new wave of single cask, limited edition, age dated and VOS and VORS Sherries can help consumers and Trade alike to disabuse themselves of the idea that Sherry is an old fashioned, inexpensive commoditised wine.

Palomino is the mainstay of Sherry production. There is no other region in the world of wine which makes so many different styles and complexities of wine from just one single grape variety.

Sherry truly is The King Of All Wines.

Appendices

Appendix

For many, many years, the worldwide trade in Sherry has been hampered, hindered and negatively affected commercially by a myriad of imitators, often of very dubious quality, passing themselves off as the real thing, and debasing the value of true Sherry. These names and places of origin have been as varied as British Sherry, Irish Sherry, South African Sherry, Cyprus Sherry, Empire Sherry, Californian Sherry, Australian Sherry and even Canadian Sherry.

Originally this can be said to be partly the fault of the authorities of Jerez themselves, for not protecting their Trade Name sufficiently assiduously in international markets rather than just in their domestic market. However as described below, various legal cases and pieces of legislation have now corrected these travesties, and the wines of the Jerez triangle are now the only wines in the world who can legally use the descriptor of Sherry.

The origins of these imitations lie in the UK, in 1905, when a Greek immigrant who picked on an idea prevalent in his homeland, that of trade in unfermented grape must which had been treated so as to prevent fermentation. His idea was to reduce the liquid of the must, to the consistency of syrup, bring it to the UK, where it would be rehydrated to bring it to a fermentable consistency, and add selected yeasts to ferment the juice to a reasonably acceptable sweet, rich, cheap alcoholic beverage. He named it British Sherry.

The trade grew exponentially after World War2, when it was considered patriotic to consume British or Empire produce, and it is probable that by around 1965, as much British and "Empire" Sherries were being sold in the UK as true Sherry.

Matters came to a head in 1967, when, in the High Court of Justice in London, the Sherry Shippers of Jerez attempted to gain a judgment preventing Vine Products the UK producer of VP British Sherry, from continuing to label their product as Sherry. Following a protracted hearing, the judge, Mr. Justice Cross delivered his verdict. Firstly he found that "Sherry" used as a stand alone descriptor could only be used to describe a wine from the Jerez district of South West Spain. However, he also found that the terms "British Sherry", "English Sherry", "South African Sherry",

"Australian Sherry", "Cyprus Sherry" and "Empire Sherry" had been used for so long without objection that it was too late to stop them now. Therefore the two camps should exist side by side. He also declared that British Sherry could be described or advertised simply as "Sherry".

This status quo remained in place in much the same way until in 1986 Spain became a member of the EU, or EEC as it was still then known. "South African Sherry" and "Australian Sherry" disappeared immediately, but "British Sherry", "Irish Sherry" and "Cyprus Sherry" were granted special dispensation to continue trading as such until 1995. Ironically, "Canadian Sherry" which has really only ever been on sale in Canada itself was permitted to continue in distribution in that country until 31st. December 2013, when the Canadian Authorities moved to outlaw it. Therefore, from a worldwide trade point of view the Producers of Sherry have only gained full nomenclature protection as from 1st. January 2014.

A remarkable situation!

Special Thanks to:

- Beltrán Domecq González and his charming wife Christine Williams, who took me under their family's wing during my early days in Jerez.

- Juan Luis Bretón, my first manager at W&H.

- Perico Bea, the export foreman at W&H who first taught me how to taste Sherry.

- Antonio Arias and Amaro de la Calle, who showed me the technical detail of Sherry making.

- Alfonso Roldán who first worked with me in the PR department at W&H and is at the time of writing is their Export Director.

- The late visionary Rafael Balao, Managing Director of Lustau in Jerez in my early days. Rafael was the inspiration behind the revolutionary Lustau range of Almacenista Sherries.

- Beltrán Domecq Williams, Cesar Saldaña, Inmaculada Menacho and the whole team at The Consejo Regulador in Jerez.

- Javier Hidalgo, President of Bodegas Hidalgo – La Gitana.

- Jan Pettersen CEO of Bodegas Fernando Rey de Castilla.

- Manuel José Valcárcel, Technical Director of Bodegas Fundador.

- The late Manuel Lozano, Oenologist at Bodegas Lustau.

- Federico Sánchez-Pece, export manager at Lustau.

- Mauricio González-Gordon, Antonio Flores, José Manuel Pinedo, Mauricio González-Gordon, Martin Skelton, Melissa Draycott and Claire Marie Henderson, all of González Byass.

- Eduardo Ojeda, Ignacio López de Carrizosa, Jaime Gil, Silvia Menacho and José Luis Monje of Grupo Estévez.

- Montse Molina and Tim Holt of Bodegas Barbadillo.

- Cristina, Paola and Rafael Medina of Williams & Humbert.

- Enrique Montero, Viticulturist with both Barbadillo and Williams & Humbert.

- Sergio Luque and Miguel Lara of Rancho de la Merced for all their help on viticultural matters and for giving me access to their rootstock and clonal research archives.

- Pelayo García of Bodega Delgado Zuleta.

- José Manuel Anelo of Álvaro Domecq S.L.

- José (Pepe) Blandino Bodega Foreman at Bodegas Tradición

- Rocío Ruiz of Bodegas Urium.

- Juan Carlos Gutiérrez, his charming wife Carmen and their daughter Carmen of Bodegas Gutiérrez Colosia.

- Fernando Hidalgo of Emilio Hidalgo S.A.

- Ana Cabestrero of Bodegas El Maestro Sierra.

- Peter Dauthieu Jr. of Viniberia Jerez.

- Marcos Aguacil, master blender at Bodegas Osborne.

- Manuel González, owner of Bodegas González Obregón

- Edmundo Grant, owner of Bodegas Grant.

- All of those at WSET who have helped me on this journey, most notably:

- Colin Gurteen, Gareth Lawrence, David Wrigley, Ian Harris and Janet Bangs to name but a few, but a heartfelt thanks to ALL the team who have supported me at both Five Kings House and the Bermondsey Street offices.

- Special thanks especially to Victoria Burt MW, as well as Karen Douglas and Nick King, all of WSET who have helped enormously in the proof reading of my text.

- Angeline Bayly and all her team at The Sherry Institute of Spain in the U.K.

- David Bird MW who has helped me greatly with technical matters of chemistry and wine technology.

- Jonathan Pedley MW, another source of solid support in matters of biochemistry.

- A special mention also to Phil Reedman MW, whom I have known for years, but who, at a chance meeting in London in 2012 suggested to me that a book of this sort was needed for Sherry – and thus set me on my way!

- Not forgetting Ron Phillips, my Spanish Master at school, who effectively lit the flame, and encouraged me hugely to speak the language properly.

- Particular thanks also to my Photographer Carlos Bellido-Flores, and Graphic Designer Max Hill, both of whom have delivered a huge amount of enthusiasm, energy and skill to the creation of this book.

- Finally, but certainly not least, my amazingly supportive wife Bernie, who has been unstinting in her encouragement throughout the planning, researching and writing of this book.

Bibliography

I could never have written this book without reference to some of the most learned writings on wine in general, and on Sherry in particular.

My thanks to all of the following:

Consejo Regulador de Jerez –Xérès – Sherry: **Sherry Wines**

Consejo Regulador de Jerez – Xérès – Sherry: **The Big Book of Sherry Wines**

Domecq Williams, Beltrán: **El Jerez y sus Misterios**, EH Editores, Jerez, 2011

Domecq Williams, Beltrán: **Sherry Uncovered**, Ediciones Presea, Cádiz, 2013

García de Luján, Alberto: **La Viticultura del Jerez**, Ediciones Mundi Press – 1997

González Gordon, Manuel: **Sherry the Noble Wine**, Quiller Press, 1990

Jeffs, Julian: **Sherry**, Faber and Faber, 1992

Liem, Peter and Jesús Barquín: **Sherry, Manzanilla and Montilla:** Manutius Press New York 2012

Radford, John: **The New Spain**, Mitchell Beazley, 2004

Robinson, Jancis: **Vines, Grapes and Wines**, Mitchell Beazley, 1986

Robinson, Jancis: **The Oxford Companion to Wine**, Oxford University Press - 1994

Domecq Williams, Beltrán: **Ageing of sherry under flor**, International symposium on viticulture, vinification and treatment and handling of wine; Masters of Wine, Oxford 1982

Hervé Alexandre : International Journal of Food Microbiology – **Flor Yeasts of Saccharomyces cerevisiae – Their ecology, genetics and metabolism** - August 2013:

C. Pardo Calle, M.M. Segovia Gonzalez, P. Paneque Macias, C. Espino Gonzalo Spanish Journal of Agricultural Research 2011 9(3) eISSN: 1695-971-X: **An approach to zoning in the wine growing regions of "Jerez-Xérès-Sherry" and "Manzanilla-Sanlúcar de Barrameda (Cádiz, Spain).**

E. Martínez de la Ossa, L. Pérez and I. Caro: American Journal of Enology and Viticulture Vol. 38, No. 4 1987: **Variations of the Major Volatiles Through Ageing of Sherry.**

P.Martínez, M.J. Valcárcel, L Pérez, T. Benítez: American Journal of Enology Vol. 49, No. 3, 1998: **Metabolism of Saccharomyces cerevisiae Flor Yeasts During Fermentation and Biological Ageing of Fino Sherry: By-products and Aroma Compounds**

Index